The

NATIONAL
PARKS

of

UTAH

A JOURNEY
TO THE
COLORADO PLATEAU

by

Nicky Leach

SIERRA PRESS
MARIPOSA, CA

DEDICATION

This book is dedicated to fellow writer Richard Mahler, a kindred spirit who understands the power of the word to stir the soul, silence to soothe it, and dance to celebrate its journey. Thanks for the editorial assistance. Te quiero, salsero. —N.L.

ACKNOWLEDGMENTS

A big thank you to Riley Mitchell and Lee Kreutzer at Capitol Reef, James Woolsey and Jan Stock at Bryce Canyon, Ron Terry and Tom Haraden at Zion, Paul Henderson at Canyonlands, and Diane Allen at Arches, who took time out of busy schedules to share information and ideas. Tim Graham and Jayne Belnap at the Biological Resources Division of the U.S. Geological Survey in Moab, whose important work on invertebrate pothole life and cryptobiotic soil crusts, respectively, inspired me to look deeper at the desert. And, as always, special thanks to publisher extraordinaire and travel buddy Jeff Nicholas for a creative and personal friendship that gets better with each passing year. —N.L.

FRONT COVER
Delicate Arch, sunset, Arches National Park.
PHOTO© ROBERT HILDEBRAND

INSIDE FRONT COVER
Mesa Arch, Island in the Sky District, Canyonlands National Park, sunrise. PHOTO© ROBERT HILDEBRAND

TITLE PAGE
Mule's ears and Temple of the Sun, Capitol Reef National Park. PHOTO© ROBERT HILDEBRAND

PAGE 4 (BELOW)
Utah juniper below Nefertiti Rock, Park Avenue, Arches National Park. PHOTO© JACK DYKINGA

PAGE 4/5
Waterfalls at Emerald Pools, Zion Canyon, Zion National Park. PHOTO© TOM TILL

PAGE 6/7
Colorado River seen from the White Rim, sunrise, Canyonlands National Park. PHOTO© TOM TILL

PAGE 7 (LOWER RIGHT)
Hoodoos, Zion National Park. PHOTO© JEFF D. NICHOLAS

CONTENTS

THE COLORADO PLATEAU

Thors Hammer and distant Aquarius Plateau, Bryce Canyon.   PHOTO© JEFF D. NICHOLAS

The Utah deserts and plateaus and canyons are not a country of big returns, but a country of spiritual healing, incomparable for contemplation, meditation, solitude, quiet, awe, peace of mind and body. We were born of wilderness and we respond to it more than we sometimes realize. We depend upon it increasingly for relief from the termite life we have created.—Wallace Stegner

It is an early July evening at Green River Overlook in Canyonlands National Park's Island in the Sky District. The smooth sandstone boulder beneath me still radiates warmth from today's 100-degree scorched sunlight. It is peaceful up here on this 6,000-foot headland. There's not a human being in sight. The silence is so deep, I can hear my heart knocking inside its bony cage.

Two enormous resident ravens call to each other from across the canyon, debating the best place to find supper, their stereophonic caws amplified and echoing in the still air. One flies up to where I sit, strutting like a tuxedoed waiter. It bows and scrapes in front of me, iridescent blue-black feathers ruffling slightly on the cooling evening canyon winds. Beak half-open, it stops in mid-sentence to look me over. The breeze stirs the yellow waving wands of prince's plume and dislodges a fragile butterfly resting on a petal. A ground squirrel scuttles over the rocks, airy tail aloft, searching for seeds.

In a wing beat the raven departs and the squirrel disappears into a crevice. I am left alone to contemplate the timeless scene in front of me, which challenges the mind to understand its scope. Sheer, thousand-foot sandstone cliffs drop straight down only inches from my boot tips to a broad plain of hard White Rim Sandstone, where a primitive, 100-mile trail has been blazed by early cattle ranchers and uranium miners. Below the protective layer of the White Rim is another series of sandstone and siltstone terraces that step back sharply into labyrinthine river canyons carved by the Colorado and Green Rivers.

It's hard to believe that erosion by the Colorado River and its siblings has created this tangled topography. Hard to believe in water out here at all in a land that receives an average of 8-10 inches

of rainfall a year, much of it in violent summer storms and winter snows, with many hot, dry months in between. But there they are—the Green and the Colorado—confluencing below the headland on which I sit, thrashing in whitewater through Cataract Canyon to Lake Powell, and moving through a series of dams to the Gulf of California, where, exhausted, the once mighty Colorado slows to a trickle and dumps its load of sediments on a muddy Mexican delta.

Many believe the Grand Canyon to be the Colorado River's masterpiece. For me, though, the real heart and soul of Canyon Country is Canyonlands National Park—a magical place of reorganized strata and river-sculpted landforms: anticlines, monoclines, buttes, mesas, benches, looping meanders, natural bridges, and volcanic mountains. There are no crowds, no developed facilities. I set up a tent in a primitive campground, truck in my own water and food, and hike trails marked by cairns in the Needles and Island in the Sky Districts absorbing 100-mile vistas.

The experiences I have had in Canyon Country were among the most magical in my life. Awakening to snow-dusted red-and-white pinnacles in the Needles one early November morning. Encountering mountain lion and deer tracks in the Arches National Park backcountry. Introducing Zion to a childhood friend visiting from England and watching her fall in love with it, as I did 20 years ago. Safely watching a flashflood from the cliffs above Horseshoe Canyon in the Maze District of Canyonlands. Getting lost in a remote slot canyon in Grand Staircase–Escalante National Monument, with little water and food, and learning the value of prayer and calm thinking to find my way out.

I have learned from all these experiences and been changed by them. This land cares not a fig for me, but I care for it. It's strangely satisfying to encounter nature on its own terms, to learn to love places, as with people, for simply being themselves. It is the essence of healthy relationship.

Utah's national parks offer a remarkable opportunity to build healthy relationships with landscapes very different from those most of us know. The five national parks have common themes—sedimentary rocks, uplift, and erosion—but each park offers variations

Turret Arch through North Window, Arches National Park. PHOTO© MARK & JENNIFER MILLER

The Narrows of the Virgin River, Zion National Park. PHOTO© ROBERT HILDEBRAND

on those themes that make them unique destinations. Canyonlands' four distinctive districts encompass carved mesa tops, interior river canyons, and lush grasslands used by humans for millennia. The world's greatest concentration of natural sandstone arches are found in Arches National Park. Capitol Reef protects the Waterpocket Fold, a 100-mile-long wrinkle in the earth's crust bisecting south-central Utah. Bryce Canyon is the spectacular setting of thousands of carved limestone hoodoos that throng the Pink Cliffs, along the eastern edge of the Paunsaugunt Plateau. Zion National Park's 2,000-foot sandstone cliffs are the highest in the world—the work of the lushly vegetated Virgin River, as it eats its way through the 10,000-foot Markagunt Plateau en-route to Lake Mead.

These parks do not exist in isolation. They are simply the headliners in an all-star cast of public lands—national monuments, national forests, wilderness areas, and state parks—that cover 11 million acres of the 83 million-acre Colorado Plateau, the mile-high geological province that contains the Colorado River System and encompasses parts of Utah, Arizona, New Mexico, and Colorado.

Along with Grand Canyon National Park in Arizona, the southern Utah parks form what is dubbed the Grand Circle, each within a day's drive of one another. The landscape is so extraordinary, though, it can become overwhelming fast. Trapped inside a car for long hours, the senses narrow down and become dull. It's easy to disconnect and not have any personal experience of the places you visit. The world beyond the windshield starts to look the same—rocks, and more rocks. The kids complain. Life becomes one mad dash from one scenic overlook to the next.

It need not be this way. The key to enjoying Utah's national parks is to do your homework before you leave, make choices, and be proactive—not passive—about your vacation. This requires some self-examination. What attracts you the most? What activities do you want to engage in? Do you want to be around other people or have some time alone, staring into space?

If you enjoy driving and bicycling scenic roads and short hikes with the family among beautiful rock formations, with developed facilities nearby, consider Bryce Canyon, Zion, and Arches National Parks. Prefer solitude and the challenge of adventure travel on backcountry trails in rugged desert country? Head for Capitol Reef and Canyonlands National Parks. Don't have much time? Choose one or two parks and get to know them intimately over several days. Go out on a trail in the early morning or evening and glimpse desert wildlife. Sign up for a ranger talk or hike. Come back when the crowds of summer are gone.

I first saw Utah's national parks 21 years ago. I have returned many times since. When I want to be awestruck by rock and space, I go to Canyonlands. When I want to be embraced by water, vegetation, and redrock canyons, I go to Zion. We are privileged in this country to have so much that is beautiful and intact made available to us whenever we need it. In turn, we must come to such places with an open heart, willing to enter into an intimate relationship with the wild. "The desert, the real desert," wrote Randall Henderson, publisher of *Desert Magazine* and an early explorer of Canyonlands, "is a land whose character is hidden except to those who come with friendliness and understanding." Welcome, friends.

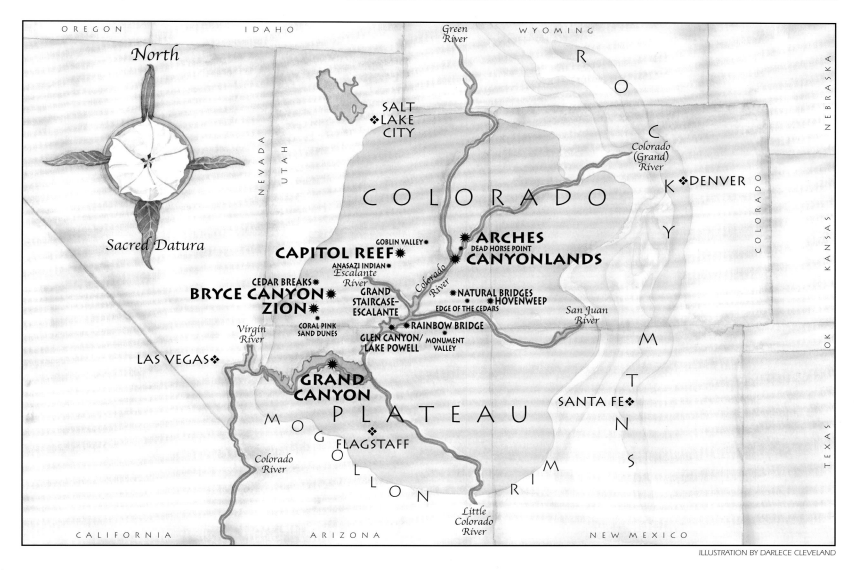

OREGON IDAHO WYOMING

North

NEVADA UTAH

Green River

Sacred Datura

SALT LAKE CITY

COLORADO

Colorado (Grand) River

DENVER

NEBRASKA

GOBLIN VALLEY

CAPITOL REEF

ARCHES
DEAD HORSE POINT
CANYONLANDS

ANASAZI INDIAN
Escalante River

Colorado River

CEDAR BREAKS

BRYCE CANYON
ZION

GRAND STAIRCASE-ESCALANTE

NATURAL BRIDGES
HOVENWEEP
EDGE OF THE CEDARS

San Juan River

Virgin River

CORAL PINK SAND DUNES

RAINBOW BRIDGE

GLEN CANYON/
LAKE POWELL

MONUMENT VALLEY

LAS VEGAS

GRAND CANYON

SANTA FE

PLATEAU

M O G O L L O N   R I M

FLAGSTAFF

Colorado River

Little Colorado River

CALIFORNIA ARIZONA NEW MEXICO

KANSAS COLORADO OK TEXAS

M O U N T A I N S

R O C K Y

ILLUSTRATION BY DARLECE CLEVELAND

It was Civil War veteran and explorer Major John Wesley Powell, the first man to conduct surveys of the Colorado River and the neighboring region in 1869 and 1872, who named the Colorado Plateau. Powell realized the high block of land was a separate geological province composed of relatively flat-lying sedimentary rocks that, unlike neighboring mountainous regions, has been relatively undeformed by volcanic activity.

The Colorado Plateau averages 5,200 feet in elevation, roughly a mile high, and has been rising gradually, about an inch a year, starting 65 million years ago, when compressions along ancient boundary faults extended the land, then twisted it around and squeezed the land in between. The 130,000-square-mile Colorado Plateau is mostly located in Utah, with small portions in Colorado, New Mexico, and Arizona. On the south, its boundary is the 2,000-foot-high Mogollon Rim, the basaltic highland that transects north-central Arizona and southwest New Mexico. Its eastern boundary is the region west of Colorado's Rocky Mountains and their southern extension—the Sandia and Sangre de Cristo Mountains—along New Mexico's Río Grande rift valley. On the north, the boundary is Utah's Uinta Mountains. The western boundary is entirely in Utah and follows the Wasatch Mountains near Salt Lake City south, past the High Plateaus of central Utah, to the Grand Wash Cliffs.

As the name implies, the Colorado Plateau is drained by the Colorado River and its major tributaries, the Green, San Juan, Dirty Devil, and Little Colorado Rivers; together they make up 3,000 miles of river. The Colorado River begins near Colorado's Continental Divide and slips into Utah just west of Grand Junction. From here, it wanders southwest, past Moab, is joined by the Green River just south of the Island in the Sky District of Canyonlands National Park, then runs through deep, narrow Cataract Canyon for 14 miles. After exiting Cataract Canyon, the Colorado is further swelled by the San Juan River, then held back in Lake Powell by Glen Canyon Dam, at Page, Arizona. Below the dam, the river passes through the Grand Canyon, where it is joined on the east by the Little Colorado River, whose headwaters are in the White Mountains, and on the west by the Virgin River, which rises north of Zion National Park on the Markagunt Plateau. Beyond the Grand Wash Cliffs, it enters Lake Mead, Nevada, passes through Hoover Dam, then continues its journey south, through a series of dams along the Arizona-California border, and out through Sonora, Mexico, into the Sea of Cortéz (also known as the Gulf of California).

 Every year, park rangers perform more and more searches and rescues of visitors who were inadequately prepared for desert conditions or ignored their physical limits. Follow these common-sense suggestions and have a fun, safe trip.

DRESS APPROPRIATELY. Protect yourself from strong sun by wearing a broadbrimmed hat, sunglasses, and sunscreen with a protection factor of 30 or higher. Exposed skin retains heat. Cover up with breathable cotton clothing; a wet bandanna around the neck is an easy way to keep the body core temperature down while hiking. Don't forget to pack a warm coverup—temperatures drop up to 30 degrees during sudden thunderstorms. In winter, trap heat next to the body by wearing layers made of high-tech synthetic fabric or silk, wool or fleece sweaters, hats, gloves, and socks, and a warm jacket. Canyon Country trails are very rough; it's easy to turn an ankle in sandals. Wear shoes with ankle support and traction, such as hiking boots.

DRINK. A liter of water per person on short hikes; a gallon for daylong excursions. Dry air makes sweat evaporate fast, so you may not realize you're getting dehydrated before you start experiencing the symptoms of heat exhaustion (confusion, dizziness, nausea, stomach cramps), or heat stroke, a more serious scenario where the body core gets so overheated, the condition can be fatal. Insufficient water is the number one cause of all deaths in the backcountry.

EAT. When you're active, the body needs fuel as well as water or else the electrolytes in the body get out of balance, causing unpleasant symptoms not unlike heat exhaustion. Salty, high-energy snacks such as trail mix are a good choice.

TAKE IT EASY. Higher elevations in the parks can cause problems, such as tiredness, dizziness, headaches, and lack of energy, for lowlanders, no matter how fit you are. Rest often, drink lots of water, cut down on caffeine, and allow the lungs to adjust to lower oxygen levels.

WATCH THE WEATHER. High-desert weather is not hot and dry all year. Snowstorms arrive as early as September and snow banks don't melt until late May atop high plateaus and mountains. Due to topographical changes, weather is often localized: sunny and warm in one place, cold and rainy five miles down the road. Canyons with little direct sun often have ice on trails until late spring. Be particularly careful during "monsoon" season, between July and October, when heavy rainstorms saturate sandy soil fast, flashflood low-lying areas and washes, and make dirt roads impassable, even to four-wheel-drive vehicles. Don't enter narrow canyons without getting an up-to-date weather forecast from rangers. Avoid exposed promontories during lightning storms. Stay in the car, tent, or under an alcove. If caught in the open, crouch down low on all fours and "ground" yourself.

ABOVE: Colorado River seen from Dead Horse Point State Park. PHOTO© TOM TILL   **OPPOSITE:** Sunrise Point, winter sunrise, Bryce Canyon National Park. PHOTO© TOM TILL

THE GEOLOGIC STORY

Most of the time, we can't see the ground beneath our feet. Lush vegetation, manmade structures, pavement, and large bodies of water hide it. But on the arid Colorado Plateau bare rock dominates. Preserved deep within its canyons and high atop its mesas is a compelling geological story: a saga of sedimentation, volcanic uplift, and erosion over vast periods of time.

Canyon Country's sedimentary rocks—sandstone, siltstones, and limestones—were laid down in a succession of oceans, near-shore environments, streams, and sand dune deserts. Each succeeding layer compressed the one below, cemented it with minerals, and hardened it into horizontal stone beds thousands of feet thick, which subsequent uplift and erosion have uncovered.

It is the sculpting action of water that has revealed the beauty in the stone heart of the Colorado Plateau. Between 6 and 1 million years ago, the Colorado River began to be affected by the much earlier uplift of the Colorado Plateau. It steepened its gradient, downcut deep, winding canyons in soft sandstone, and carried away tons of sediments to the Gulf of California. The deepest carving can be seen in the Grand Canyon, where the river has exposed 1.8 billion years of the earth's 4.56 billion-year history. To the north, some 300 million years of earth history is on display in Utah's five national parks, all of them set aside for their unique geology.

The oldest visible rocks in Utah are located in Westwater Canyon, the Colorado River canyon adjoining Canyonlands National Park. Canyonlands and neighboring Arches National Park sit in the large Paradox Basin, a trough that formed during the **Pennsylvanian Period**, 320 to 286 million years ago, when volcanic activity pushed up the Uncompahgre Uplift just to the east, in the vicinity of the present-day La Sal Mountains. Throughout the Pennsylvanian and **Permian Periods**, a span of 100 million years, the climate in the Southwest was warm and tropical. Western America

was located roughly where West Africa is today, the result of the earth's continents drifting on a sea of red-hot magma below the earth's surface and moving into their current positions.

An enormous shallow ocean covered the West. In southeastern Utah's Paradox Basin, the sea was intermittent, often drying out, and leaving behind salt beds thousands of feet thick. The Paradox salt formation was gradually buried by red, iron-rich sediments washed down from the Uncompahgre Uplift and white sand dune deposits laid down in a coastal plain environment when the sea withdrew. These red and white deposits hardened into the Cutler Group—the White Rim Sandstone, Organ Rock Shale, Cedar Mesa Sandstone, and Elephant Canyon Formation/Halgaito Shale—which have eroded so beautifully into banded spires in the Needles District. In Zion National Park, inundation by the Permian Sea was more consistent and laid down Kaibab Limestone, the oldest rock in that park. The Kaibab was formed as, over time, marine creatures died in the sea, piled up on the sea bottom, and their fossils fused into a hard reef cemented by calcium carbonate precipitated from sea water.

Canyonlands' basement-level Paradox salt formation may be invisible now, but it has influenced the entire southeastern Utah landscape. If, even when you are sitting still, you could swear the landscape is in motion, don't be surprised. It has been for millennia. Compressed by thousands of feet of later sediments, the Paradox salt flows away from the overburden, escaping along faults in the rock, and heaving up the landscape into salt domes. These salt domes eventually crack, allowing groundwater to enter, dissolve the salt, and cause the rocks to collapse. On the east side of the Colorado River, below its confluence with the Green, salt has caused fault blocks to drop into corridors known as grabens. In the Salt and Cache Valleys in Arches National Park, uplift and collapse of salt domes created cracks in the 200-million-year-old overlying Entrada Sandstone. The ongoing freeze-thaw action of groundwater and

the "flushing out" of sand grains by rainfall then sculpts fins and refines some into arches, which themselves collapse as gravity takes over.

The most visible formations on the Colorado Plateau were laid down during the **Triassic** and **Jurassic Periods**, 245 to 144 million years ago. Early in the Triassic, highlands throughout southern Utah had been reduced by erosion to hills whose sediments—clays, silts, sand, and pebbles—filled mountain basins, giving us the soft, crumbly vermilion Moenkopi Formation and banded purple-gray Chinle and Morrison Formations. The latter contain uranium, which, in the 1950s, lured many miners to Canyonlands in search of big government payoffs. Another treasure in the Chinle is petrified wood, the preserved remains of huge conifers that fell into streams, were entombed in volcanic ash and mud, and had their wood cores turned to quartz by silica-rich groundwater.

Sandstone is instantly recognizable by its beautiful reddish hues, uniform texture, and ability to weather into sheer cliffs. During the Jurassic Period, 208 to 144 million years ago, the earth's climate experienced a long, hot, drying trend. Much of the West was buffeted by blowing sands that piled into enormous dunes that were crossbedded as the wind changed direction. The towering orange Wingate Sandstone found in Canyonlands' Island in the Sky District and along the Fremont River in Capitol Reef were deposited during this time. Between the dunes were shallow pools and streams, a favorite haunt of dinosaurs, whose tracks are often seen in the ledgy maroon Kayenta Formation siltstone that settled out in the still water. A few million years later, desert conditions returned, creating the 150,000-square-mile Navajo Desert and sand dunes more than 3,000 feet high. When the land was once again inundated by a marine environment that left behind iron and lime, the dunes hardened into salmon-hued Navajo Sandstone. The Navajo

Sandstone is a familiar sight, but reaches its greatest beauty and thickness in the 2,000-foot cliffs carved by the North Fork of the Virgin River through Zion Canyon.

Iron rusts Zion's rocks dramatically and changes hue as it is washed down through the sandstone. Iron and manganese are also responsible in part for desert varnish, the distinctive, shiny red, brown, and black streaks that tapestry sandstone walls. Desert varnish is believed to be caused by a combination of minerals, blowing clay, and dust that are fixed on the dripping cliff faces by resident bacteria and microfungi.

One of the most aesthetically pleasing marriages of form, color, and water erosion occurs at Bryce Canyon National Park, where streams coursing off the steep east side of the 9,000-foot Paunsaugunt Plateau have carved thousands of hoodoos, or oddly eroded rocks, in the Pink Cliffs. These pastel-tinted sedimentary rocks are some of the youngest in Utah. They were deposited as limestone, mudstone, and sandstone in a large lake during the **Tertiary Period**, 50 to 60 million years ago, creating a 1,300-foot-thick layer dubbed the Claron Formation. The Claron is soft and easily eroded, with rocks of different types yielding to gravity in their own way. Mudstone crumbles into terraces, limestone into columns, with caps of erosion-resistant dolomite keeping the whole thing standing, until it, too, falls away.

You can't travel anywhere on the Colorado Plateau without being aware of volanic activity. As recently as a million years ago, volcanic eruptions spewed lava flows atop the Markagunt Plateau. Canyonlands is bounded on the east and southwest by intrusive volcanoes that never broke the surface. Dubbed laccoliths, they include domed mountains like the Henrys, the Abajos, and the La Sals, whose granitic cores have slowly been uncovered by erosion. The Rocky Mountain Uplift, which occurred 65 million years ago, was the most important seismic event in Utah's geological history. Crustal movements along California's San Andreas Fault reverberated throughout the West, pushing up the Rockies and the Colorado Plateau, as well as a host of contorted geological features.

One of the most contorted features is the Waterpocket Fold, technically a monocline, which dominates south-central Utah and is preserved in Capitol Reef National Park. The Waterpocket Fold runs for 100 miles from Thousand Lake Mountain to Lake Powell and is especially dramatic on its southern tip, where it rears into a jagged cockscomb of red Kayenta and white Navajo strata tilted skyward. The Fold's north end is very different. Here, the Fremont River has carved a 1,000-foot-deep passageway through sandstone cliffs, creating an important riparian oasis and travel corridor used by wildlife and humans for millennia.

Southwestern Utah's plateaus appeared a mere 10 to 15 million years ago, when the release of pressure along faults caused the Markagunt, Paunsaugunt, Kaibab, Kaiparowits, and Paria Plateaus to split and rise above the parent Colorado Plateau. These soaring tablelands have been sculpted into a 5,000-foot-high geological "Grand Staircase," ascending northward in a series of colorful, tiered cliffs from the Grand Canyon through Zion to Bryce Canyon. The individual formations form a color-coded sequence. They are, in order: the Chocolate Cliffs, the Vermilion Cliffs, the White Cliffs, the Gray Cliffs, and the Pink Cliffs.

HUMAN HISTORY

Much of southern Utah is so remote, it feels like virgin territory. It's all an illusion. Human beings have used even the remotest canyons in southern Utah for at least the last 11,500 years and have left many clues to their presence.

The first people here trod very lightly on the land. Paleo-Indian hunters arrived on the North American continent via the Bering Land Bridge at the end of the Ice Age, pursuing woolly mastodons, camels, giant bison, and ground sloths across the savannah grasslands that then existed on the Colorado Plateau. The hunters moved with the big-game herds, slept in cave shelters, flaked stone tools, and butchered onsite, leaving behind occasional bones, stone flakes, and beautiful chert spear points of a type known as Clovis and Folsom.

Big-game herds vanished as the climate became more desertlike and they were hunted to extinction. Humans, however, adapted. They became nomadic hunter-gatherers who moved seasonally, from southwest Utah's high plateau country to the deepest canyons in southeastern Utah, harvesting seed-bearing grasses, nuts, and other wild foods. They hunted bighorn sheep, rabbits, and other small game with spear-throwers known as atlatls. These Archaic people lived within the dictates of the land, moved often, and thrived for a very long time in southern Utah, from about 6,000 B.C. to A.D. 500.

But late in the Archaic period, there are indications that things started to go wrong, perhaps triggered by drought and diminishing natural resources. Archaic hunters began leaving split-twig hunting fetishes of game animals in high ledges in canyons, probably to ensure a good hunt. Deep in the Maze District of Canyonlands, life-size images of limbless, hollow-eyed, ET-like beings were painted on sand-

stone walls. Otherworldly and haunting, they seem the overheated visions of shamans making long pilgrimages to sacred sites in order to call on higher powers for help.

That help may never have come, for in A.D. 500, Archaic people were trying something new: the cultivation of a domesticated grass introduced from Mexico called corn. Agriculture did more than revolutionize the way prehistoric Southwest people ate; it changed their whole world view. Families stayed in one place beside water sources, planted and tended fields, and were soon joined by extended clan members who helped with the work load. Greater leisure time led to an explosion in creativity, as people shared ideas, experimented with building techniques, traded with neighbors, and perfected another new invention from Mexico—pottery—which, with its reliance on local soils and individual decorations, now indicates who lived where on the Colorado Plateau.

The most popular houses in this desert climate were circular, underground pithouses. These were cool in summer and warm in winter, with roofs made of branches covered in earth and held up by central supports. People of the northern Colorado Plateau, the Fremont, never abandoned this type of house. Nor did they give up the nomadic Archaic hunting and gathering lifestyle on the high plateaus, along the Fremont and Escalante Rivers, and in the canyons of Capitol Reef, San Rafael Swell, and the Kolob area of Zion. Indeed, Fremont rock art, with its spectacular panels of red trapezoidal anthropomorphs and zoomorphs, and unique, slit-eyed female clay fertility fetishes, has strong Archaic echoes.

The best-known prehistoric people were the Ancestral Puebloans, whose stone villages were first encountered by Spanish explorers across the southern Colorado Plateau in 1540. The Pueblo people started out as pithouse dwellers like the Fremont but soon began building hamlets, then larger villages of aboveground, multistory, masonry homes set next to fertile floodplains along Colorado River tributaries. The Virgin Anasazi homeland extended from the Virgin River in Zion National Park perhaps all the way east to the Escalante Canyons. Similarities in painted pottery and architectural style indicate the Virgin Anasazi may have been a branch of the Kayenta Anasazi, who, in the 1200s, built magnificent cliff dwellings preserved at Navajo National Monument in northern Arizona. Southeastern Utah's rugged topography slowed settlement. By the 1200s, though, even remote canyons like Salt Creek in Canyonlands National Park had attracted homesteaders who built small, hidden homes and granaries high in alcoves. By 1300, the entire Four Corners had been abandoned, probably as a result of a long drought,

ABOVE: Horseshoe Ruin, Hovenweep National Monument. PHOTO© JEFF D. NICHOLAS

floods, overpopulation, diminishing resources, and internal pressures. Clan after clan left and moved in with other Pueblo people along the Río Grande in New Mexico and the Little Colorado and Gila Rivers in Arizona, building what are today's Zuñi, Hopi, and other pueblos.

Just as the Ancestral Puebloans were leaving, a new people were spreading into southern Utah from southern California. Numic-speaking Southern Paiutes arrived in the 1100s and learned corn farming from Puebloans, but were most at home wandering seasonally across defined territories marked by family-owned springs. They lived in brush shelters, gathered seeds, piñon nuts, and other plants in finely woven baskets, harvested and roasted agave (considered a sacred food), and snared, netted, and bow-hunted deer, rabbits, even bear, on high plateaus in Zion, Cedar Breaks, and Bryce Canyon. The first recorded European contact with the Southern Paiute came in late 1776, when members of the Shivwits band saved the Spanish Domínguez-Escalante Expedition from potential starvation when it was forced to turn back near Cedar City and return to Santa Fe, New Mexico, via the Grand Canyon.

Spanish slave raiding and introduced diseases reduced Paiute numbers, but most devastating was the loss of their lands to the cattle and homes of new settlers, who arrived in southern Utah in the mid-1800s. Members of the Church of Jesus Christ of Latter Day Saints, or Mormons, had been forced to flee their homes in the Midwest, after their leader, Joseph Smith, was killed in Nauvoo, Illinois, by a mob. Using explorer John C. Frémont's recent report on western lands, church president Brigham Young led his people west, traveling thousands of miles on foot, in search of a new homeland. In 1847, the caravan reached Utah and founded Salt Lake City,

at the foot of the Wasatch Mountains. Mormons planted crops, began grazing livestock, built temporary dugout homes, then sturdy stone buildings to a consistent town plan. In a stroke of genius, they timed their arrival just in time to make a financial killing supplying miners headed for the California gold rush in 1849.

By the late 1850s, Brigham Young began "calling" his most trusted followers to colonize southern Utah and convert local Indians. The 1851 Iron Mission built southern Utah's first town, Cedar City; 10 years later, the 1861 Cotton Mission founded St. George. Southeastern Utah proved more challenging. The 1855 Elk Mission, which tried to build a settlement at the only ford across the Colorado River for miles, near modern-day Moab, was turned back by hostile Utes. Moab was eventually founded in the 1870s. Then, in the winter of 1879, members of the San Juan Mission made a foolhardy, but ultimately successful, journey across the

tangle of canyons and ridges south of Canyonlands National Park to found Bluff on the San Juan River. South-central Utah's rugged heartland, in the area of Capitol Reef, was settled late. Mormon polygamists, fleeing government persecution in the 1880s, and other Mormon settlers helped found towns along the Fremont and Dirty Devil Rivers, including Hanksville, Caineville, and Fruita—which is now preserved within Capitol Reef National Park.

American trappers risked traveling through remote areas of Utah while it was still Spanish territory in the early 1800s. Trapper Denis Julien was the first European to leave his signature in the river canyons of Canyonlands in 1838. When the area became United States territory in 1848, government surveyors arrived to map the area, including John Wesley Powell's 1869 and 1872 Colorado River surveys, which filled in gaps on G.K. Warren's first 1858 survey map of Canyon Country. Black homesteaders fled slavery and began new lives as ranchers in Moab. Cowboys drove enormous herds across open range in the 1880s, a trampling from which the grasslands have never recovered. Miners filed claims along the Colorado, the San Juan, and other rivers but found too little gold and silver to justify the expense and hard work to get their ore out. Oil, gas, and uranium mining have brought more lasting returns. Big uranium finds in Canyonlands in the 1950s lured many hopefuls to Moab until the Cold War boom turned to bust. Many of those same miners are now river guides, who take adventurous visitors into river canyons and backcountry deemed by one 1861 newspaper as "measurably valueless, excepting for nomadic purposes, hunting grounds for Indians, and to hold the world together."

ARCHES NATIONAL PARK

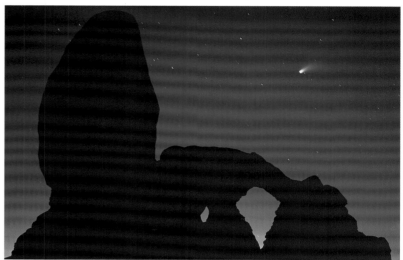

Turret Arch and Hale-Bopp Comet, Windows section. PHOTO© TOM TILL

I am seated in the shadow of an enormous Entrada Sandstone boulder in the Windows section of Arches National Park, watching the world go by and writing in my journal. A plateau lizard is sunning itself on a rock. Two cottontails just hopped past and disappeared into the blackbrush. Jays are jabbering noisily in the piñon trees, squabbling over nuts. Every few minutes, a little shower of sand blesses me from the rocks above, the quartz grains loosened gradually over time by heavy rains, frost, wind, plant roots, and animal feet.

Hikers on the trail hail me and ask how much farther it is to their destinations. Parents hand in hand with young children and trailed by bored teenagers race past, chattering and encouraging each other, mentally collecting arches and memories that will linger long after they return home. Fellow solitaries lost in reverie come around the bend, suddenly see me, and are startled from their daydreams. "Nice spot," they say, standing next to me to admire the view. "Seen anything interesting?"

Interesting? You bet. Arches is a place where nature and human beings come into contact in the most companionable way possible. It's a small, accessible piece of desert heaven, just five miles out of Moab. The most spectacular arches, fins, spires, towers, pinnacles, and balanced rocks are visited easily on short trails that radiate from either side of the paved scenic drive. You could spend a day here and, like an avid birder, check off every major arch in the park, including the world's most famous span, Delicate Arch. But this drive for quantity over quality seems futile in a place with more arches than anywhere else in the world—more than 2,000 at the last count. It's simply impossible to see them all.

And why would anyone want to? The intimacy we crave with nature cannot be rushed. When we slow down and take in the environment, carefully examine its details using all our senses, it becomes part of who we are from then on. We can plant a piece of the natural world inside our hearts, let it take root, then bring it out for examination again and again. That way, like anything we genuinely love, it stays alive. Writer Edward Abbey, who worked as a ranger in Arches during the 1950s and wrote about his experiences in *Desert Solitaire*, urges us to take the time to look deeply: "If Delicate Arch has any significance, it lies, I will venture, in the power of the odd and unexpected to startle the senses and surprise the mind out of its ruts of habit, to compel us into a reawakened awareness of the wonderful—that which is full of wonder."

I see plenty of wonder in this park. People seem to fall in love with it and truly make it their own. From where I am hidden, I spend an hour watching visitors at Double Arch. It is fascinating to see the transformation that takes place in each person. Many size themselves against its bulk, unable to believe how dwarfed they feel. A few thoughtfully rub the sandpaper graininess of the 200-million-year-old sandstone and reflect on the mystery of 100 million years of water and wind erosion. Some peer through the arch's enormous openings at the bolt-blue sky and 12,000-foot La Sal Mountains beyond, heads cocked, reframing the world as if their eyes were camera lenses. Others stand still, simply staring, smitten by rock, sky, and the unadorned magic of the moment. Scooping up huge handfuls of sand at the base of the arch, even the adults are like children playing in a sandbox, imagining the world—and their place in it—from a whole new perspective.

One's perspective in Canyon Country is always changing. To newcomers, the landscape seems huge and overwhelming. We struggle to understand the scope of this place and why it looks the way it does. Grand vistas are thrilling, excite something in us that we can barely name. We willingly lose ourselves in them, calmed, perhaps, by something so much bigger than the mind's ability to grasp it. We forget that, as someone once said, "God is in the details." A child's world seems to consist of such details, as naturalist Gary Paul Nabhan recalls in writing about a trip to the Colorado Plateau with his family in *The Geography of Childhood*: "Little did I know what my children would allow me to see: Lilliputian landscapes often overlooked by educated adults seeking the Big Picture... I realized how much time adults spend scanning for the land for picturesque panoramas and scenic overlooks. While the kids were on their hands and knees engaged in what was immediately before them, we adults traveled by abstraction."

OPPOSITE: Inside Double Arch, Windows section. PHOTO© TOM TILL   PAGE 20/21: Elephant Butte seen from Park Avenue, Courthouse Towers section PHOTO© TOM TILL

Pinnacles of the Fiery Furnace.

PHOTO© JEFF GNASS

Morning light at Broken Arch.

PHOTO© ROBERT HILDEBRAND

The Moab Panel.

PHOTO© TOM TILL

Starting back on the trail, I am caught up in the details of my immediate environment. I scan the trail for footprints and scat, wondering what passed through here last night. Coyote? Mountain lion? Canyon mouse? Most of all, I notice the strange, lumpy, brown-sugar-textured soil that forms castlelike mounds and often has plants growing out of it. This soil covers 75 percent of Canyon Country, so it's easy to overlook in favor of more exciting plants and animals and rocks. But this cryptobiotic crust, as it is known, is far from ordinary; it is alive. Composed of cyanobacteria (formerly known as blue-green algae), lichens, microfungi, mosses, liverworts, and algae, it is essential to desert country because it produces microscopic sheaths that weave throughout the top few millimeters of soil, glue particles together, and form the biological crust that stabilizes erosion. When it rains, cryptobiotic crust can expand to 10 times its size, thereby increasing water absorption—important in these arid lands. It increases soil fertility by fixing essential nutrients such as nitrogen and carbon. The mounds shelter plant seeds, providing nurseries for native plants that would otherwise be blown away by desert winds. In a very real way, crypto, as it is called informally, is the foundation for all life in the desert.

But in the last century, cryptobiotic soil has been lost at a rate not seen in the last 10,000 years. Tires, hooves, and feet crush in seconds what has taken centuries to form. Recovery can take another two centuries. Meanwhile, damaged soil is exposed to greater erosion and blows away at a faster rate than it can be replaced, exotic species like cheatgrass move in and outcompete native grasses, and shrubs and junipers invade sandy areas. The fate of cryptobiotic soil points to an unusual paradox: although this desert land seems timeless, tough, and better adapted than we, all is not as it seems. The fragile bonds that hold the landscape together are easily broken by human impacts we are only beginning to understand. Humility is required. Often the most insignificant things are the most important. Avoid cryptobiotic soil by staying on the trail or walking only in sandy washes and on slickrock. Don't bust the crust!

Educating visitors about how to avoid cryptobiotic crust is just one of many issues facing managers at Arches National Park. The park attracts some 800,000 visitors each year. On summer days, all 869 parking spaces throughout the park have been taken by 10 a.m. The Windows is so popular it has been designated a "Sensitive Resource Protection Zone," and is being monitored for vegetation damage. The small visitor center is filled to overflowing most days, testing the ability of park staff to provide the information, education, and publications that visitors require.

Despite these challenges, Arches is a park that has always inspired humans to greater things. In 1968, Ed Abbey's memoir *Desert Solitaire* was the first such book to speak on behalf of this land. In 1964, the same year that the federal Wilderness Act was passed, Arches superintendent Bates Wilson—a desert rat if ever there was one—helped get nearby Canyonlands set aside. It was an early 20th-century miner in the Klondike Bluffs area of Arches who first lobbied for that area to be designated a national park. Even crusty Civil War veteran John Wesley Wolfe, whose log cabin sits near the Delicate Arch trailhead, was hope-

Balanced Rock, Windows section, and La Sal Mountains, winter sunset. PHOTO© TOM TILL

ful. He brought his whole family to live here in the late 1800s, believing in the healing power of the desert and the chance to reinvent oneself.

A little reinvention may be necessary for some beleaguered national parks, but Arches will content itself with improving upon what it does best. Visitors are now required to register for the popular Devils Garden campground at the entrance and sign up in the visitor center for ranger-led tours of Fiery Furnace, offered daily for a small fee. The National Park Service hopes to build a large new visitor center in 2003-2004, with better exhibits and visitor facilities. Arches is looking into transportation alternatives, perhaps a voluntary shuttle system.

But nothing can change the simple joys of Arches. Strolling along Park Avenue below the Three Gossips. Standing beneath the elegant span of 306-foot Landscape Arch, one of the largest known arches in the world. Catching a glimpse of reintroduced bighorn sheep grazing in Courthouse Wash. Making a pilgrimage to Delicate Arch, whose fragile beauty is heightened by the drama of its slickrock rim setting. Here, indeed, is a world of wonders.

Landscape Arch, Devils Garden. PHOTO© CHARLES GURCHE

North

Collared Lizard

ARCHES

KLONDIKE
BLUFFS

DEVILS
GARDEN

LANDSCAPE ARCH ✦

❖DEVILS GARDEN TRAILHEAD

SALT

SKYLINE ARCH ✦

VALLEY

❖SAND DUNE ARCH
FIERY
FURNACE

FIERY FURNACE VIEW
SALT VALLEY OVERLOOK
❖WOLFE RANCH

DELICATE ARCH
✦

NATIONAL

DELICATE ARCH
VIEWPOINT

PANORAMA POINT

TO CRESCENT JUNCTION

191

TO CANYONLANDS AND DEAD HORSE POINT

313

BALANCED ROCK ✦
ROCK
PINNACLES

THE
WINDOWS

❖GARDEN OF EDEN

❖DOUBLE ARCH
❖NORTH & SOUTH
WINDOWS

TURRET ARCH ✦

THE GREAT WALL

Courthouse

❖ PETRIFIED DUNES VIEW

128

TO CASTLE VALLEY

PETRIFIED
DUNES

PARK

Wash

SHEEP ROCK ✦   ✦TOWER OF BABEL
THREE GOSSIPS ✦   ❖COURTHOUSE TOWERS VIEW
COURTHOUSE   ❖THE ORGAN
TOWERS   LA SAL MOUNTAINS VIEW
PARK AVENUE TRAILHEAD ✦

Colorado River

VISITOR CENTER

128

❖MOAB

279

KANE CREEK
ROAD

191

TO POTASH   TO MONTICELLO

ILLUSTRATION BY DARLECE CLEVELAND

SIZE: 120 square miles. **FOUNDED:** Set aside as Arches National Monument in 1929. Upgraded to Arches National Park in 1971. **LOCATION:** From Moab, take U.S. 191 north 5 miles to park entrance. **ELEVATIONS:** 3,960 to 5,653 feet. **HIGHLIGHTS:** More than 2,000 arches, plus windows and other sandstone formations, including Delicate Arch, Double Arch, Landscape Arch, Fiery Furnace, Devils Garden, Klondike Bluffs, Courthouse Towers, Park Avenue, Balanced Rock, and the Three Gossips. **SEEING THE PARK:** Drive or bicycle the paved scenic drive from the visitor center. Road has numerous scenic pullouts and trailheads. Hiking in Arches is generally easy and highly recommended for the whole family. Balanced Rock, Double Arch, and the North and South Windows in the Windows section are all easy destinations; simply follow rock cairns along the trails. Landscape Arch and Double O Arch on the 7.2-mile Devils Garden loop are slightly more strenuous, as is 3-mile Delicate Arch Trail. Ranger-led hikes into Fiery Furnace are offered daily, between April and October, for a fee. Group size is limited to 10 people. Sign up early for these popular hikes at the visitor center. **VISITOR CENTER:** At the park entrance, off US 191. Open 8 a.m. to 4:30 p.m. daily, with extended hours seasonally. Park information, exhibits, orientation films, publications, ranger talks. Year-round water and restrooms. **VISITOR SERVICES:** Gas, food, and lodging are available in Moab. For information, stop at the multiagency Moab Information Center on Center Street and Main (open summer 8 a.m.–9 p.m.; winter, 9 a.m.–5 p.m.; tel. 435-259-1370; closed Christmas, Thanksgiving, and New Year's Day. **CAMPGROUNDS:** Devils Garden Campground has 52 tent and trailer sites and is open year round, on a first-come, first-served basis. Flush toilets and water are available year-round. Two walk-in group sites for tent campers may be reserved for 11 or more people. Contact Southeast Utah Group, National Park Service, 2282 S. West Resource Boulevard, Moab, UT 84532-8000 or fax 435-259-4285. **SPECIAL CONSIDERATIONS:** Register for Devils Garden Campground at the park entrance. Arrive early; campsites fill fast. Ranger-led hikes into the Fiery Furnace also fill quickly. Stop at visitor center to sign up. Carry a lot of water; summer temperatures reach 110 degrees! Stay on trails to avoid crushing cryptobiotic soil, the dark soil crust essential to plant life in the desert. **PARK CONTACT INFORMATION:** Superintendent, Arches National Park, P.O. Box 907, Moab, UT 84532-0907; 435-719-2299 or www.nps.gov/arch.

OPPOSITE: Delicate Arch, sunset. PHOTO© RANDY A. PRENTICE

BRYCE CANYON NATIONAL PARK

Natural Bridge.
PHOTO© JEFF D. NICHOLAS

Many of southern Utah's landscapes stretch the very limits of credulity. Places like Canyonlands and the Grand Canyon are so big, so awe-inspiring in their landforms, that one could spend several lifetimes getting to know them. Others, though, seem human-scaled and understandable on first viewing, their extraordinary geology accessible to ordinary mortals.

Bryce Canyon is such a place. In this high-country park, water pouring over steep limestone cliffs has sculpted one of the Southwest's most intriguing landscapes: a series of natural amphitheaters scooped out of the east face of the Paunsaugunt Plateau, then carved into fairytale tableaux of sunset-hued fins, spires, arches, bridges, windows, turrets, and weathered pinnacles known as hoodoos.

Fifteen spectacular viewpoints jut out from three different coniferous forests along Bryce Canyon's 18-mile scenic drive. Each view is like a framed Technicolor diorama with fantasy scenes reminiscent of a Cecil B. De Mille movie epic: batallions marching, weapons waving, crowds cheering, queens presiding. Released from their nightly enchantment by the early morning shadows of the dawn, they seem, as geologist Clarence Dutton put it in 1880, "the work of giant hands, a race of genii, once rearing temples of rock, but now chained up in a spell of enchantment."

The Southern Paiute, who hunted and gathered here seasonally for centuries, also thought Bryce Canyon's hoodoos were enchanted. "Before there were any Indians, the Legend People, *To-when-an-ung-wa*, lived in that place," a Paiute called Indian Dick explained in 1936. "Because they were bad, Coyote turned them all into rocks. You can see them in that place now; some standing in rows; some sitting down; some holding onto others. You can see their faces, with paint on them, just as they were before they became rocks . . . The name of that place is *Agka-ku-wass-a-wits* (Red Painted People)."

Paunsaugunt, Markagunt, Panguitch, Paria, Yovimpa, and other Paiute names seem fitting in a landscape that engages rather than defies the imagination. But names like Sunrise, Sunset, and Inspiration Points capture what is most enduring about Bryce Canyon: its timeless beauty.

Viewpoints in the Bryce Canyon Amphitheater loop are closest to the visitor center and have the heaviest traffic and crowded parking lots. But between May and September visitors have the option of parking at the shuttle parking-and-boarding area and riding a free shuttle into the park and this area. Buses run every 10-15 minutes and stop at overlooks, as well as the visitor center, Bryce Canyon Lodge, and the General Store. The paved Rim Trail connects the Bryce Canyon Amphitheater overlooks. When you're ready to leave, simply hop onto another bus.

From the Paunsaugunt Plateau, on a clear day, you can see for 100 miles. To the east are the dizzying sandstone labyrinths of Grand Staircase–Escalante National Monument and Glen Canyon National Recreation Area; the hidden Colorado, San Juan, Escalante, and Dirty Devil Rivers; the little-visited Henry Mountains, south of Hanksville; and humpbacked Navajo Mountain, sacred to the Navajo whose reservation lies nearby.

I arrive in Bryce Canyon late one fall evening, passing mule deer grazing roadside amid vivid yellow sunflowers and fuzzy rabbit-brush. I hope to glimpse one of the threatened Utah prairie dogs protected in the park, or perhaps a yellow-bellied marmot waddling sleepily out of the forest. The only rodents I encounter, though, are assertive little squirrels and chipmunks, who plead with big eyes for a handout. For their good, and mine, I walk on.

I set up camp in Sunset Campground beneath tall ponderosa pine trees that sway gently in the breeze. Their platey bark exudes a comforting vanilla smell that reminds me immediately of the forests surrounding my old home in Flagstaff, Arizona. I am filled with nostalgia. In the lower elevations, bright desert sunlight exposes every nook and cranny, blows the cobwebs from my mind. But in the cool high-country forests, I feel something deeper, beyond thoughts and words. Perhaps it's the Green Man, the pagan spirit of the European woodlands, speaking in the forgotten language of trees.

My reverie is interrupted by a symphonic crash of timpani thunder ricocheting from rock to rock. The danger of lightning strikes brings hikers running from exposed rims back to camp. As

Douglas fir in Wall Street.

PHOTO© ROBERT HILDEBRAND

The Silent City as seen from Inspiration Point, sunrise.

PHOTO© TOM TILL

night falls, small campfires flicker in hearths in many campsites. A Mexican family sings ballads accompanied by a guitar while children run around and grownups laugh. Climbing into my sleeping bag in the back of the truck, with a good book and a mug of cocoa, I let their melifluous voices lull me to sleep as the rain starts to beat a faint tattoo on my roof.

Early the next morning, I join knots of visitors descending the 1.3-mile Navajo Loop. Hikers fill water bottles, then disappear below the rim, following short but steep trails that make the knees quiver going in and the heart pump fast in the thin, high-country air, coming out. With little vegetation to slow erosion on the cliffsides, they quickly crumble into badlands as intermittent streams and creeks pour off the rims and join the Paria River below. The town of Tropic was founded at the base of the cliffs in 1891, but it was an earlier homesteader along the Paria River who gave the park its name. Mormon pioneer Ebenezer Bryce ran cattle through a canyon below the Pink Cliffs for five years, starting in 1875. Bryce had already pioneered several communities by the time he arrived here, and southern Utah's spectacular scenery may have started to pall. An apocryphal story has it that Bryce once commented that the canyon was simply "a hell of a place to find a cow that was lost."

Bryce Canyon National Park encompasses not a single canyon, but many. On the Navajo Loop Trail, I pass through Wall Street, a narrow slot canyon, where cerulean sky barely peeks from behind high castellated walls. There is enough shade and moisture here to support Douglas firs, which yearn skyward toward the sun. As the canyon opens out and sunlight bores back down on me, piñon, juniper, and ornate-looking greenleaf manzanita appear among boulders, forming rock gardens that invite contemplation. Except for the breeze playing through the canyon and the occasional loud bickering of pinyon jays over seeds, it is silent here.

The trail switchbacks through pale Claron Formation limestone laid down in a freshwater lake, 55 million years ago, shortly after the dinosaurs died and the Rocky Mountains were appearing. The elevation of the Colorado Plateau trapped the lake within highlands, which shed sand, clay, and silt into the waters. When the lake evaporated, these sediments compressed into sedimentary rocks cemented by calcite precipitated from mineral-rich water. Iron and manganese delicately tinted the rocks: phosphorescent oranges, reds, yellows, and browns from iron; purples, pinks, and blues from manganese.

The high plateaus of southwestern Utah were formed 15 million years ago, when the land began to rise again along faults. The Paunsaugunt Plateau is the top step in the Grand Staircase, a 5,000-foot-high geological formation made up of the eroded cliff faces of the tiered plateaus, extending from Bryce Canyon to Grand Canyon. Each plateau preserves sedimentary rocks that make up, in descending order, the Pink Cliffs, the Gray Cliffs, the White Cliffs, the Vermilion Cliffs, and the Chocolate Cliffs. It's thought that, at one time, rocks found at Bryce Canyon may have covered the rimrocks of the Grand Canyon. Erosion has stripped them away.

Bryce Amphitheater seen from Sunset Point, winter sunrise.

PHOTO© J.C. LEACOCK

The focal point of Bryce Canyon is erosion. Uplift that split the land into plateaus also fractured the watermelon-hued limestone into joints. As slightly acidic rainwater enters these cracks, it dissolves the calcite cementing the rocks, creating pathways for sediment-laden streams to downcut channels and ridges called fins. Water erosion, abetted by the more than 200 nights of freeze-thaw at this high elevation—along with the actions of wind, plant roots, animal feet, and gravity—gradually form windows, arches, and natural bridges. The hoodoos themselves appear when the holes in the rocks widen and their tops narrow. It's only a matter of time before the whole formation crashes down, leaving behind thousands of columns that differing levels of erosion then shapes into hoodoos. The famous landmark of Thors Hammer is one among thousands. It looks like a tool used by one of Dutton's "genii," with a squared anvil head capped by hard dolomite and a handle molded from softer silt and claystone.

Thors Hammer can be seen north of the Navajo Loop. Just beyond, I pick up the 1.4-mile Queens Garden Trail and huff and puff my way up to Sunrise Point. Near the top, I overtake a family from Washington D.C. with whom I visited in Zion National Park a few days earlier. They have fallen in love with Canyon Country and are on one last hike before heading home via Las Vegas, Nevada, a few hours southwest of here. People love Bryce, but rarely is it a destination in itself. Instead, like America's version of Europe's 18th-century Grand Tour, this park usually forms one of several scenic stops on southern Utah's famous Grand Circle.

Bryce has welcomed visitors from all over the world since the early 1900s, when Ruby's Inn founder Ruby Syrett built his first lodging, Tourists Rest, near the rim and had guests sign in by carving the front door. In the 1920s, architect Gilbert Stanley Underwood designed a series of rustic "parkitecture" lodges for new parks at Zion, Cedar Breaks, and Bryce Canyon. Of these, only Bryce Canyon Lodge survives—its wavy-shingled roof, log-and-stone construction, casement windows, beamed dining room, and Twenties-era furnishings completely renovated in 1988, and echoed in the park's rehabilitated visitor center, opened in fall 2001.

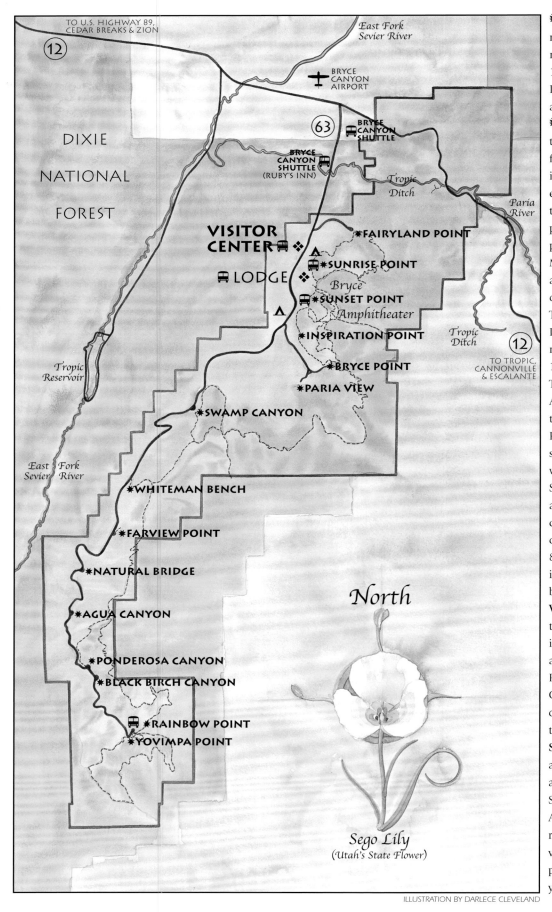

TO U.S. HIGHWAY 89,
CEDAR BREAKS & ZION

12

East Fork
Sevier River

BRYCE
CANYON
AIRPORT

63

BRYCE
CANYON
SHUTTLE

DIXIE

NATIONAL

FOREST

BRYCE
CANYON
SHUTTLE
(RUBY'S INN)

Tropic
Ditch

Paria
River

VISITOR
CENTER

LODGE

✱FAIRLAND POINT

✱SUNRISE POINT

Bryce

✱SUNSET POINT

Amphitheater

✱INSPIRATION POINT

✱BRYCE POINT

✱PARIA VIEW

Tropic
Ditch

12

TO TROPIC,
CANNONVILLE
& ESCALANTE

Tropic
Reservoir

✱SWAMP CANYON

East Fork
Sevier River

✱WHITEMAN BENCH

✱FARVIEW POINT

✱NATURAL BRIDGE

✱AGUA CANYON

North

✱PONDEROSA CANYON

✱BLACK BIRCH CANYON

✱RAINBOW POINT
✱YOVIMPA POINT

Sego Lily
(Utah's State Flower)

ILLUSTRATION BY DARLECE CLEVELAND

SIZE: 56 square miles. **FOUNDED:** Protected as a national forest in early 1900s. Set aside as a national monument in 1923. Upgraded to a national park in 1924. **LOCATION:** From west, take U.S. 89, south of Panguitch, to junction with Utah 12. Follow Utah 12 and 63 to park entrance. Commuter airport on Utah 12. **ELEVATIONS:** Rim: 8,000 feet at park entrance rising to 9,115 feet at Yovimpa Point. Below the Rim: 6,600 feet. **HIGHLIGHTS:** 14 natural amphitheaters containing arches, bridges, fins, spires, and hoodoos carved by erosion in the eastern face of the Paunsaugunt Plateau, the Pink Cliffs. 15 scenic viewpoints. Three forest types: piñon-juniper, ponderosa, spruce-fir and bristlecone pine. **SEEING THE PARK:** 18-mile paved scenic drive. Mountain biking. Concessionaire-run horseback rides and scenic air tours outside the park. Snowshoeing and cross-country skiing in winter. Nine hikes. 11-mile Rim Trail (easy) links the scenic overlooks; 8-mile Fairyland Loop has views into Fairyland and Campbell Canyons near park entrance; 1.3-mile Navajo Loop (moderate), 1.4-mile Queens Garden (easy), and 5.5-mile Peekaboo Trails (moderate-strenuous) descend into Bryce Canyon Amphitheater; 1-mile Bristlecone Loop (easy) wanders through spruce-fir forest to a bristlecone outcropping at Rainbow Point; 0.8-mile Mossy Cave (easy) is a streamside walk, northwest of Utah 12, to a mossy grotto and waterfall; 23-mile Under-the-Rim Trail and 9-mile Riggs Spring Loop Trail offer strenuous backcountry hiking (fee and permit required). **VISITOR CENTER:** Park headquarters and visitor center open daily, year-round, except Thanksgiving, Christmas, and New Year's Day. Hours 8 a.m.–8 p.m. (summer); shorter hours in winter. Park information, exhibits, publications, orientation film, backcountry permits, lost and found. **VISITOR SERVICES:** Historic 114-room Bryce Canyon Lodge and restaurants, open mid-May to November 1. Gas, food, lodging just outside park available year round. Post office and general store open in park seasonally; year-round at Ruby's Inn. **CAMPGROUNDS:** North and Sunset Campgrounds have 216 campsites, available on a first-come, first-served basis. One group campsite by reservation only. Winter camping available. **SPECIAL CONSIDERATIONS:** Voluntary shuttles operate between May and September. Blue Shuttle connects Park and Ride stops along Highway 63 with visitor center inside park. Blue Shuttle connects with Red Shuttle for Bryce Canyon Amphitheater Loop. Green Shuttle offers daily limited runs to Yovimpa Point. Reservations required. Inquire at visitor center. **PARK CONTACT INFORMATION:** Superintendent, Bryce Canyon National Park, Bryce Canyon, UT 84717; 435-834-5322. www.nps.gov/brca.

OPPOSITE: Cliffs glowing in early morning light, Agua Canyon. PHOTO© TOM TILL

CANYONLANDS NATIONAL PARK

Sunrise from Maze Overlook, Maze District.　　PHOTO© TOM TILL

The squawking raven perched on my tent poles wakes me at 5:30 a.m. Bleary from yesterday's eight-hour drive from Santa Fe, I thank him for the wakeup call through clenched teeth and yawn. Rolling over, I disentangle myself from the sleeping bag, dress quickly, and step out into the delicious coolness of a July morning in the Needles District of Canyonlands National Park.

Dawn among these 300-million-year-old rocks feels primordial, as if I am the first human being to witness it. The sun rising in the east backlights the Six Shooter Peaks and Abajo Mountains. To the northeast, I can see the La Sal Mountains, named by Spanish explorers. In English, they are the Salt Mountains, a reference to the salt deposits underlying this area. Directly north, Canyonlands' Island in the Sky District emerges from the haze like a Manhattan skyscraper, a 6,000-foot-high plateau of Wingate, Kayenta, and Navajo Sandstone carved by the converging Green and Colorado Rivers. To the south, out of sight, are Comb Ridge, the Bears Ears, Natural Bridges National Monument, and the San Juan River. To the west, also hidden, are the formations known as the Needles and the Grabens, and beyond them, the Colorado River and the tangled canyons of the Maze, on the other side of the river.

Canyonlands National Park is huge and wild—and that is its main attraction. It covers 527 square miles and is naturally divided into four districts by the Colorado and Green Rivers: The Needles, The Island in the Sky, the Maze, and the rivers themselves. Although connected to each other geographically, each district is a long way from the others by road, making it hard to visit more than one or two during any single trip. The single best overview of the entire park and its breathtaking geology can be had at Island in the Sky, west of Moab. Dramatic overlooks such as Grand View, Green River, and Shafer offer 100-mile views of Canyonlands from east and west of the mesa. Short trails lead to geological features and extraordinary views at Mesa Arch, Whale Rock, and Upheaval Dome, a jumble of rocks that scientists now believe may be a collapsed salt dome in a meteorite impact crater.

For a different perspective, river trips on the Colorado River led by local outfitters leave from Potash, just north of Moab, and float below the Island in the Sky, coming ashore in historic Lathrop Canyon. Here, four-wheel-drive vehicles bring passengers up to the Island in the Sky on the dirt Shafer Trail, often stopping at Musselman Arch, Monument Basin, and other awe-inspiring sights along the 100-mile White Rim Trail.

The river is also one way to enter the Maze, Canyonlands' most remote and rugged district. Canyonlands guide Kent Frost, who grew up in Monticello, was one of the first to explore the Maze in the 1950s, taking Jeeps down the Flint Trail to places he and his guests named Defiance Canyon, Land of Standing Rocks, the Doll House, and Henderson Arch. For millennia, the Maze's deepest canyons were used by wandering Archaic, Fremont, and Ancestral Pueblo Indians. In the late 1800s and early 1900s, hardy pioneer ranchers like Orange Seely ran cattle Under the Ledge, as the area below the rim was called. In the late 1800s, outlaw Butch Cassidy and his gang hid out at Robbers Roost Ranch in the nearby San Rafael Desert, foiling all attempts to find them.

No visit to the Maze should be undertaken lightly. The most accessible hike is the 6.5-mile hike into Horseshoe Canyon to view 5,000-year-old Barrier Canyon-style pictographs left behind by the Archaic culture. But even this trip requires preparation, as Horseshoe Canyon is 30 miles from Utah Highway 24 on a dirt road that washes out when it rains.

For adventurous yet relatively safe hiking and four-wheel-driving above the river, nothing beats the Needles. My sandy campsite beneath the piñon and juniper in the Squaw Flat Campground is private and cozy. I am surrounded by cliffs and canyons, interspersed with native grasslands, creeks, and springs that, until the 1970s, were used by local cowboys. Many of these cattlemen were based at the historic Dugout Ranch, rancher Al Scorup's old place on Indian Creek, immediately east of the park. Their line camps dot the Needles. One, preserved by the park service at Cave Creek, contains stacked wood, horse feed boxes, kitchen items, cupboards, and homemade rustic furniture, in a cave with permanent dripping springs and a panel of Indian pictographs. Ancestral Pueblo dwell-

Cottonwood in Horseshoe Canyon, autumn.   PHOTO© ROBERT HILDEBRAND

Pictograph panel known as "Thirteen Faces", Needles District.   PHOTO© TOM TILL

ings, granaries, and rock art panels blend into alcoves in side canyons like Salt Creek and Peekaboo, and throughout the Needles. These structures were built by members of an offshoot of the Mesa Verde culture in the 1200s but were abandoned within the century, probably because of a long drought, diminishing resources, and social reorganization.

I boil water for tea, eat a bowl of cereal, and pack nuts, apples, and a liter of water into my backpack. I know that if I want to hike I must leave now, before 100-degree summer heat bores down on the open desert. Hopping in the car, I drive west to the 7-mile Chesler Park Trailhead, the best day hike in the Needles. The trail is reached via a narrow, gravel road that winds down through Cutler Formation rocks that erosion has sculpted into odd toadstools. At any moment, I expect to stop and ask directions of a caterpillar smoking a hookah, so Alice-in-Wonderland is the scene. I park at Elephant Hill, and start the short, steep climb on a well-maintained but rough trail into massive, jointed rocks. A hawk is uttering a high-pitched shriek from a clifftop perch as it scans the flats for cottontails, jackrabbits, and other prey. I look up, hoping to catch sight of it, but the bird has moved to new hunting grounds.

Above the rim of the canyon, I am in full sun. The temperature shoots up 15 degrees. I start sweating and stop to drink water. Cairns lead the way across slickrock. They are so similar to natural rocks that it's easy to miss one, go the wrong way, and find yourself rimrocked. I slow down to make sure I don't lose my bearings. I also try to tune into the way the land rises and falls, twists and turns, checking my own intuitive directional sense against that of the trail builders. This internal hiker pulls me inexorably forward, one foot in front of the other, using a deeper intelligence. Sounds, smells, and sights become more intense. I feel myself relax and grow confident in my route-finding skills. I pass a father and son returning from Chesler Park. The father is offering a running commentary on desert hiking; the boy, probably around 13 years of age, seems apprehensive but excited to be out alone with his dad. He tugs the straps of his backpack nervously and looks around, awestruck by a world that offers so few touchstones for modern city dwellers.

The trail moves through a narrow slot between two fins, where even the gentlest footsteps echo loudly. On the other side, the trail passes through a piñon-and-juniper "garden." Then it crosses the sandy Elephant Canyon wash and ascends into grassy meadows and the red-and-white-banded, eroded spires of the Needles. If I wanted to make a long day of it, I could continue on the Joint Trail and loop back to the trailhead or back to Elephant Canyon, hiking along the wash to 200-foot-high Druid Arch, named for its resemblance to Stonehenge. Longer explorations require a permit, a backcountry campsite reservation, and time to wander for a few days into the 300-feet-deep Grabens, where brittle sandstone has been yanked along by moving underground salt and massive blocks have dropped between faults along the Colorado River. A hiking trail descends Lower Red Lake Canyon to the river, where you can see Spanish Bottom, in the Maze on the opposite bank.

Angel Arch and Molar Rock in Salt Creek Canyon.   PHOTO© TOM TILL

Monument Basin and distant Abajos from Grand View Point.   PHOTO© JEFF D. NICHOLAS

Native grasslands in the Needles District.   PHOTO© TOM TILL

The Colorado River with Island in the Sky visible in background.   PHOTO© TOM TILL

I turn back at the Needles and return to my campsite to break camp. On the way out, I stop at the visitor center. Rangers tell me that the upper section of Salt Creek will remain closed to vehicles indefinitely, and the lower section open to only a few private vehicles by permit, so great are the concerns about damage to riparian vegetation and invertebrates that live in the creek. When the park was set aside in 1964, about 18,000 Jeeps a year entered Canyonlands, most driven expertly by folks like Kent Frost who had grown up in this country. In 2000, a whopping 500,000 Jeeps were counted, far more than fragile desert lands can bear. More than ever, the National Park Service, charged by law with providing access AND preventing impairment of the resource, must steer a middle course between access and preservation.

In the human hierarchy, decisions about ecosystem management come from the top down. In the natural world, ecosystem recovery is a bottom-up affair. New research at Salt Creek indicates that this may already be occurring. In the summer of 2001, field studies in the closed areas carried out by the U.S. Geological Survey's Biological Resources Division and Earthwatch volunteers, under contract to the National Park Service, showed that ant farming of aphids is producing sugar water beneath exotic clovers once grazed by cattle. This "honey dew," as it is called, in turn, attracts cicadas, and their predators, spiders, an important species in the recovery of the Canyonlands ecosystem. Small beginnings, to be sure. Yet significant ones.

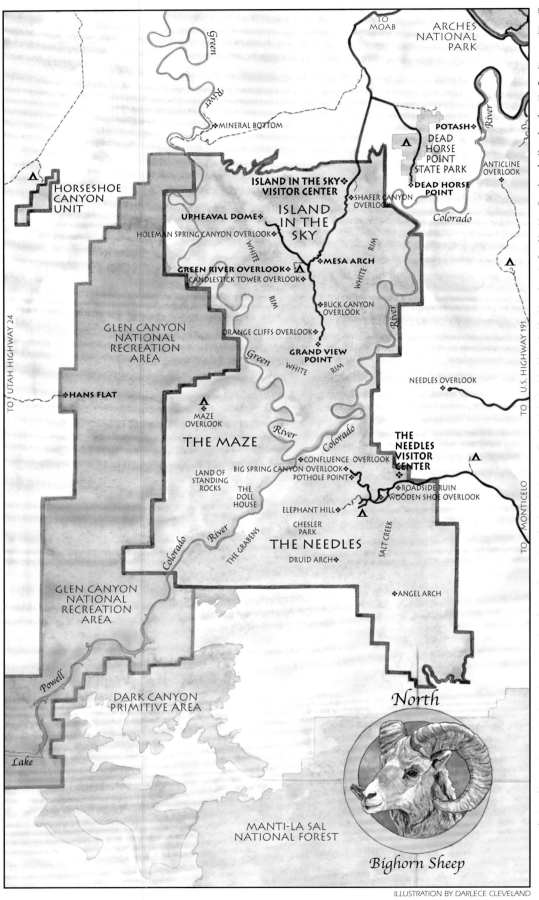

HORSESHOE CANYON UNIT

TO MOAB

ARCHES NATIONAL PARK

Green

River

River

MINERAL BOTTOM

POTASH

River

DEAD HORSE POINT STATE PARK

ANTICLINE OVERLOOK

ISLAND IN THE SKY VISITOR CENTER

SHAFER CANYON OVERLOOK

DEAD HORSE POINT

UPHEAVAL DOME

ISLAND IN THE SKY

Colorado

HOLEMAN SPRING CANYON OVERLOOK

WHITE RIM

GREEN RIVER OVERLOOK

MESA ARCH

CANDLESTICK TOWER OVERLOOK

WHITE RIM

RIM

BUCK CANYON OVERLOOK

River

GLEN CANYON NATIONAL RECREATION AREA

ORANGE CLIFFS OVERLOOK

Green

GRAND VIEW POINT

WHITE RIM

NEEDLES OVERLOOK

HANS FLAT

River

Colorado

MAZE OVERLOOK

THE MAZE

LAND OF STANDING ROCKS

CONFLUENCE OVERLOOK

BIG SPRING CANYON OVERLOOK

POTHOLE POINT

THE NEEDLES VISITOR CENTER

THE DOLL HOUSE

ROADSIDE RUIN

WOODEN SHOE OVERLOOK

ELEPHANT HILL

CHESLER PARK

Colorado

River

THE GRABENS

THE NEEDLES

SALT CREEK

DRUID ARCH

GLEN CANYON NATIONAL RECREATION AREA

ANGEL ARCH

Powell

DARK CANYON PRIMITIVE AREA

North

Lake

MANTI-LA SAL NATIONAL FOREST

Bighorn Sheep

TO UTAH HIGHWAY 24

TO U.S. HIGHWAY 191

TO MONTICELLO

ILLUSTRATION BY DARLECE CLEVELAND

SIZE: 527 square miles. **FOUNDED:** Canyonlands National Park was set aside in 1964, then expanded in 1971, with the addition of Horseshoe Canyon in the Maze District. **LOCATION:** To reach Island in the Sky, drive west from Moab for 32 miles on U.S. 191 and Utah 313; The Needles is 76 miles southwest of Moab, via U.S. 191 and Utah 211. The Maze District is reached via Utah 24, south of Green River. Colorado River trips start from Potash Road, just west of Moab. **ELEVATIONS:** 4,000 to 6,000 feet. **HIGHLIGHTS:** Dramatic vistas of mesas and convoluted river canyons cut by the Colorado and Green Rivers. **SEEING THE PARK.** The most accessible district is 6,000-foot-high Island in the Sky, near Moab, which has fabulous views of the Paradox Basin and pleasant day hikes to Mesa Arch and Upheaval Dome. The dirt Shafer Trail switchbacks to the 100-mile White Rim Trail, popular in spring with mountain bikers and four-wheel-drivers. The 4,000-foot-elevation Needles District is hotter and offers a backcountry experience amid grasslands, banded spire rocks, and canyons east of the Colorado River. Hikes include Chesler Park, Druid Arch, Elephant Canyon, the Grabens. Challenging 4WD routes over Elephant Hill lead toward the river. The Maze District is remote and difficult to negotiate. Most accessible is the 30-mile sandy road to the rock art panel at Horseshoe Canyon. River trips can be arranged through concessionaires in Moab. **VISITOR CENTER:** Moab Information Center in downtown Moab has general information (for details, see Arches chapter). Visitor centers at Island in the Sky and the Needles are open year-round 8 a.m. to 4:30 p.m., with extended summer hours. The Hans Flat Ranger Station in the Maze is 45 miles from Utah 24. **VISITOR SERVICES:** Nearest gas, food, ice, and airstrip to The Needles is Needles Outpost at the park boundary, and Monticello. Nearest services to Island in the Sky are in Moab. Nearest services to the Maze are in Hanksville and Green River. **CAMPGROUNDS:** Primitive 13-site Willow Flat Campground at Island in the Sky; no water. Squaw Flat Campground in The Needles has 26 sites, toilets, and water between April and Sepember. Designated backcountry campsites available by reservation throughout the park. **SPECIAL CONSIDERATIONS:** Carry food and at least a gallon of water per person per day, spare tires, and emergency vehicle repair gear. **PARK CONTACT INFORMATION:** Superintendent, Canyonlands National Park, 2282 S. West Resource Boulevard, Moab, UT 84532; 435-259-7164; www.nps.gov/cany.

OPPOSITE: Barrier Canyon-style pictographs of the Great Gallery, Horseshoe Canyon. PHOTO© TOM TILL

CAPITOL REEF NATIONAL PARK

The Henry Mountains seen from Upper Muley Twist.   PHOTO© JEFF D. NICHOLAS

I am in love with Capitol Reef National Park. Like many relationships, it didn't happen quickly, and now it surprises me with its intensity. As with people, sometimes I am drawn to a place slowly, discovering its beauty and charms on my own terms and in my own time. With Capitol Reef, it was worth the wait.

Courtship is different for others, of course, depending on one's interests and ways of looking at the world. Photographers, for example, may look at the 100-mile-long Waterpocket Fold, the huge wrinkle in the earth's crust preserved in Capitol Reef, and be inspired by the rainbow breakers of sandstone crashing like a frozen ocean from Thousand Lake Mountain to Lake Powell. They might trek to the same spot at dawn every morning, waiting for precisely the right light on the vermilion "mummy cliffs" at Chimney Rock. On other days, driving to the park from the nearby town of Torrey, they may be struck by nature's sense of order in the Chinle Formation—the way junipers and piñons seem to grow evenly spaced as if planted by a landscape designer in a garden of the gods.

A painter, on the other hand, may prowl the narrow canyons and set up an easel next to a single Indian paintbrush or bee flower. Such a visitor might look intensely at the flower's stamens or the folds of its petals, then have these take center stage on canvas. Both photographer and artist look beyond surfaces and seek to portray the spirit of what they are seeing—an impossible task, perhaps: "Nobody sees a flower, really," New Mexico painter Georgia O'Keeffe once admitted. "It is so small—we haven't time, and to see takes time, like to have a friend takes time."

Seeing, really seeing, does takes time. And who has enough time these days? We are hungry for connection, but in our rush for instant gratification, we take shortcuts that leave us more lost than when we started. One day, though, something shifts. We make the choice to slow down, to give ourselves a chance to connect on a more personal, intimate level with our surroundings, and to stop "hoarding our spirit," as Utah writer Terry Tempest Williams puts it. Suddenly, the commonplace is revealed for what it is: everyday magic, available to us anytime we allow ourselves to fall under its spell. The late

writer Ward Roylance, whose Entrada Institute headquartered in Torrey is dedicated to educating visitors about the region, understood such enchantment. To him, Capitol Reef was always "The Enchanted Wilderness."

A visit to Capitol Reef National Park begins on Utah Highway 24 in the northern section of the Waterpocket Fold. The winding highway follows a deep gorge cut by the Fremont River, a major waterway lined with preternaturally green grass, cottonwoods, and willows that contrast dramatically with overhanging 1,000-foot pink Wingate Sandstone cliffs. The Navajo Sandstone atop the cliffs has been molded by erosion into domes, buttes, pillows, and knobs that melt into an electric blue sky. Abandoned adobe and log structures built by 19th-century Mormon settlers nestle at the base of the cliffs. Signs along the road invite visitors to stop and pick apples, cherries, peaches, pears, and apricots from the pioneer orchards in season. Trails and backcountry roads to Chimney Rock, Hickman Bridge, and Cathedral Valley take off from pullouts north of the highway; south of the road are trails to Cohab Canyon and Grand Wash, one of several narrow side canyons that cut through the Waterpocket Fold, emerging at the 20-mile round trip scenic drive, south of the visitor center.

The massive warp in the earth's crust known as the Waterpocket Fold is a monocline, an enormous north-south-oriented geological step. Between 50 and 70 million years ago, movements along an ancient buried fault pushed the rocks 7,000 feet higher on the west than on the east. Erosion then stripped away much of the overlying sedimentary layers. Today, the oldest strata are found in the western part of the park; the youngest at the eastern boundary, where they form the crumbly eerie badlands around Notom-Bullfrog Road and Caineville. The drama of the monocline is softened by river erosion in its northern district. On the south, though, north of Lake Powell, it's a different story. Here, the violence of the seismic episode that created this enormous buckled landform cannot be hidden. Standing below the huge tilted shelves of sandstone on Burr Trail Road, the old rancher's route across the Fold, I am aware of the powerful forces that continue to shape the land. I feel amazed, humbled, and

Early morning in Upper Cathedral Valley.   PHOTO© JEFF D. NICHOLAS

Fremont Culture petroglyphs near the Fremont River.   PHOTO© TOM TILL

Orchards in bloom, Fruita Historic District.   PHOTO© TOM TILL

very, very small.

The Waterpocket Fold is not unique. The Colorado Plateau has more monoclines than anywhere else in the world. Nor are the 14 different rock formations found in the 250-million-year-old cliffs unusual; sedimentary rocks similar to these are found throughout southern Utah. Deposition of sediments, hardening of rock, uplift, and erosion of sandstone by rivers, wind, and other forces is a story oft repeated in this desert land. But what is special is the way all these features combine so spectacularly in Capitol Reef. Moreover, the presence of the Fremont River and other perennial streams within the high, sculpted recesses of the Waterpocket Fold accounts for the park's enormous biological diversity. Within feet of each other are various ecological niches created by the juxtaposition of slope, water, exposure, and elevation. Different soil types attract specific plants. Many endemic plant species are found here, including six rare plants that are federally listed as endangered or threatened species, or are candidates for such listings.

Capitol Reef has a long human history. The Waterpocket Fold was named by explorer John Wesley Powell for pockets in the rocks that fill with life-giving water during rainstorms. Later settlers called it Capitol Reef because its rocky ramparts were a barrier to travel and its smooth domes were reminiscent of the roof of the U.S. Capitol. During the 1880s, government raids on Mormon polygamists in southern Utah led several families to take refuge in these hidden canyons. They put down roots and founded the town of Junction, later renamed Fruita. Elijah Behunin built a simple adobe house south of the river on the east side of the park. Once isolated, it now sits beside Utah Highway 24, a poignant reminder of the hardy, self-sufficient ranchers and farmers who once made lives in this remote spot.

At least six different communities were founded along the Fremont River over a period of 100 years, but periodic floods and droughts made living hard and frustrating. Residents gradually drifted away. Part of the present national park was originally proposed as Wayne Wonderland State Park in the 1930s. In 1937, it received federal recognition as a national monument. Capitol Reef National Park was set aside by Congress in 1971, with Fruita as park headquarters. Today, the abandoned pioneer settlement retains much of its historic charm. Sprinklers irrigate lush grass in the shady picnic area and campground, providing a welcome respite from 100-degree summer heat. The 200-acre Fruita Rural Historic District preserves the 1896 Schoolhouse, 1908 Gifford Homestead, Blacksmith's Shop, and historic orchards containing roughly 3,000 fruit trees, the most extensive in the National Park System.

The orchards are a reminder that Fruita was an important fruit-growing center, supplying settlers all over south-central Utah. Customers included Robert Parker, alias Butch Cassidy, who traveled here frequently from his hideout at Robbers Roost, east of the park. Cassidy carved his signature on the wall of a side canyon, along with many other early miners, surveyors, explorers, and settlers. A number of inscriptions are preserved at the Pioneer Register in Capitol Gorge, a narrow side canyon that, until Utah Highway 24 was built in 1962, served as the main road through the Waterpocket Fold. The earliest historic signatures are those of two prospectors who passed through in 1871.

Also found in Capitol Gorge (and along Highway 24) are thousand-year-old petroglyphs incised by prehistoric Fremont people who lived along the Fremont River between A.D. 700 and 1250. These first residents of Capitol Reef cultivated fields of hardy corn along the fertile floodplain and stored crops in granaries in side canyons. They hunted bighorn sheep and deer and made a unique moccasin from deer hide, using a deer's dewclaw for traction on the heel. Their early pottery was a distinctive, unpainted black or gray ware, with raised or tooled surfaces. Later, they began to decorate this grayware with black paint—similar to Mesa Verde ceramics— possibly as a result of contact with Ancestral Pueblo neighbors to the south.

But, though they had much in common with their Pueblo neighbors, the Fremont lifestyle harkened back to the successful hunter-gatherer traditions of the area, perhaps as a result of living in well-watered highlands with plenty of game and food-providing plants. They continued to build pithouses on game migration routes and appear to have used fetishes ceremonially. "Anatomically correct" female, slit-eyed clay figurines have been found secreted in ledges, perhaps to ask their gods for fertility. The Fremont seem to have understood the value of magic.

When I explore Capitol Reef, I am rewarded with many magical moments. The reflections of a changing sky in a water-filled pothole atop the Waterpocket Fold move my heart unexpectedly. A conga line of chukars blocking traffic on a dirt canyon road makes me laugh out loud. Rain, that dreary fixture of my British childhood, is now something I celebrate in arid desert lands, where rainfall may only measure 8-10 inches a year. After a late afternoon thunderstorm, my eyes are dazzled by the reds, oranges, pinks, greens, yellows, and browns that make up what the Navajo call "The Land of the Sleeping Rainbow". The pungent odor of sagebrush wrinkles my nostrils. Spadefoot toads awaken from underground torpor beneath potholes atop the Fold and mate with wild abandon. The air is soft, washed clean. Standing atop a rock on the Cohab Canyon Trail, it feels like the dawn of creation.

Basalt boulders and badlands of the Bentonite Hills.　PHOTO© JEFF D. NICHOLAS

Boulder near Egyptian Temple, along Scenic Drive.　PHOTO© JEFF D. NICHOLAS

FISHLAKE NATIONAL FOREST

CATHEDRAL VALLEY

SOUTH DESERT

WATERPOCKET

TEMPLE OF THE SUN✧

FACTORY BUTTE✧

UTAH 24 TO BICKNELL

FRUITA HISTORIC DISTRICT
1896 FRUITA SCHOOLHOUSE
PETROGLYPH PANEL
HICKMAN BRIDGE
CAPITOL DOME

TO HANKSVILLE

24

Fremont   River

✧TWIN ROCKS
Creek
PANORAMA POINT✧ ✧CHIMNEY ROCK
GOOSENECKS OVERLOOK✧   ✧THE CASTLE
TORREY

✧CAINEVILLE

RIVER FORD

VISITOR CENTER✧

Fremont   River   Grand Wash   BEHUNIN CABIN

North

12

SCENIC DRIVE

Capitol Gorge

NOTOM

Mountain Bluebird

DIXIE NATIONAL FOREST

▲SINGLETREE
Creek

FOLD

BULLFROG

Pleasant

▲PLEASANT CREEK
Oak   ▲OAK CREEK
Creek   Creek

ROAD

CEDAR MESA
▲

WATERPOCKET

✧ANASAZI INDIAN STATE PARK
BOULDER
TRAIL

TARANTULA MESA

GRAND STAIRCASE–

BURR   ROAD

ESCALANTE

FOLD

LOWER MULEY TWIST TRAILHEAD✧ ✧
THE POST

TO ESCALANTE AND BRYCE CANYON

▲ CALF CREEK

12

NATIONAL

Escalante

BURR

TRAIL

MONUMENT

HALLS CREEK OVERLOOK✧ ✧

River

GLEN CANYON

NATIONAL

RECREATION

AREA

ROAD

TO GLEN CANYON NRA (BULLFROG MARINA)

ILLUSTRATION BY DARLECE CLEVELAND

☀**SIZE:** 378 square miles. ☀**FOUNDED:** Set aside as Capitol Reef National Monument in 1937. Upgraded to Capitol Reef National Park in 1971. ☀**LOCATION:** From east or west, take Utah 24. From south and Bryce Canyon, take Utah 12. ☀**ELEVATIONS:** 3,875 to 8,800 feet. ☀**HIGHLIGHTS:** The 100-mile-long Waterpocket Fold in south-central Utah, including Capitol Dome, Capitol Gorge, Grand Wash, the Fremont River, Cathedral Valley, Fruita, the Burr Trail, Muley Twist Canyon, and Notom-Bullfrog Road. ☀**SEEING THE PARK:** Utah 24 offers a highly scenic 15-mile-roundtrip drive through the upper section of the Waterpocket Fold. Historic Fruita preserves the Gifford Homestead, a Blacksmith's Shop, more historic orchards, and shady picnic grounds. The 10-mile scenic drive follows the western portion of the Waterpocket Fold south to Capitol Gorge and Pleasant Creek Ranch. Short hiking trails include Cohab Canyon, Capitol Gorge, Grand Wash, Cassidy Arch, and Hickman Bridge. East of the Fold, off Utah 24, 4WD routes head north to Cathedral Valley, in the South Desert. Remote backcountry routes through starkly eroded Entrada Sandstone and Morrison Formations. Washouts are common. Check on road conditions at the visitor center before starting out. Access to the southern section of the park is via Utah 12 to Boulder, then the paved Burr Trail Road to the park boundary, where the road is unpaved and crosses the Fold via dramatic switchbacks. Hikes in the southern section include a difficult, multiday hike through the slot canyon of Halls Creek Narrows and several day hikes, 2 to 24 miles in length. East of the Fold, the Burr Trail Road joins Notom-Bullfrog Road, the scenic dirt road running east of the Fold from Utah Highway 24 to the Bullfrog Marina on Lake Powell. ☀**VISITOR CENTER:** Park headquarters is in Fruita. The visitor center is open daily from 8 a.m. to 4:30 p.m. and offers information, exhibits, ranger talks, publications, and reproduction Fremont Indian and Mormon pioneer handicrafts. ☀**VISITOR SERVICES:** There are no visitor services in the park. The closest gas, food, and lodging is in nearby Torrey, west of the park. ☀**CAMPGROUNDS:** Fruita Campground has 70 sites; Cedar Mesa and Cathedral Valley Primitive Campgrounds have 5 and 6 sites, respectively. ☀**SPECIAL CONSIDERATIONS:** This park is remote. Plan any trip here carefully and carry food, water, and spare emergency roadside gear. Note that most tourist facilities in Torrey close between October and April. ☀**PARK CONTACT INFORMATION:** Superintendent, Capitol Reef National Park, Torrey, UT 84775; 435-425-3791 or www.nps.gov/care.

OPPOSITE: Upper Cathedral Valley, late-afternoon. PHOTO© JEFF D. NICHOLAS   PAGE 44/45: Sulphur Creek Canyon and the Waterpocket Fold, sunset. PHOTO© TOM TILL

ZION NATIONAL PARK

Crossbedded Navajo Sandstone, Zion-Mt Carmel Highway.   PHOTO© JEFF D. NICHOLAS

I arrive in Zion during the mother of all summer storms. The sudden change in atmospheric pressure creates high winds that send pale dust devils and tumbleweeds cartwheeling across the Smithsonian Butte Scenic Backway, a shortcut through the Vermilion Cliffs. My truck thermometer reports a 30-degree temperature drop outside, from 90 to 60 degrees in 30 seconds, as I drive directly below the storm cell into the Virgin River Valley. At 6 p.m. it is so dark I can't see more than a few feet in front of me. I turn my headlights on.

Not far from here, in 1880, John Wesley Powell's surveyor, the eloquent geologist Clarence Dutton, stood atop the Vermilion Cliffs and viewed for the first time the spectacular Zion and Parunuweap Canyons carved by the North and East Forks of the Virgin River. "In an instant," marveled Dutton, "there flashed before us a scene never forgotten. In coming time it will, I believe, take rank with a very small number of spectacles each of which will, in its own way, be regarded as the most exquisite of its kind, which the world discloses. The scene before us was the Temples and Towers of the Virgin."

Today, those Temples and Towers are wreathed in cumulonimbus storm clouds marshaling their forces into a single army of uniform gray walling the northern horizon. Lightning tears across the forested pedestal of 7,000-foot-high West Temple, near Zion's South Entrance, leaving behind a ghostly jagged halo. As I cross the Virgin River on the single-lane bridge into Rockville, I look down into the frothing, sediment-laden floodwaters of earlier upcountry storms. The river hisses and roars over boulders like an angry snake, as it breaks up and devours the 260-million-year-old rocks of the southern Markagunt Plateau. This is a river that is still relatively untamed, a powerful foe in flood, as prehistoric and Mormon settlers discovered again and again. It is both creator and destroyer of everything here. The Paiutes call it *Par'us*, or "whirling water." Spanish explorers named it the Virgin—and it truly is a miracle in this desert.

At the little town of Virgin, just off Highway 9, I turn north up the Kolob Reservoir Road into the high country of the Kolob Plateau, Zion's quieter northwestern section. I will camp tonight in the primitive Lava Point Campground, the jumping-off point for the West Rim Trail that joins Zion Canyon on the east with the Kolob Canyons unit of the park on the west, via the Kolob Terrace. Temperatures at this 7,900-foot elevation are cooler in summer, a respite from the fiery 100-degree walled-in heat down in the 4,000-foot valleys. Today's storm is a "gully washer," one of several storms that will knock out power in Zion Canyon every night during my stay.

Within minutes, the sluicing rain has abated. The setting sun hits the Navajo Sandstone cliffs, creating a delicate rosy flush in the iron-rich rocks. It takes only a few minutes for groundwater moving down through porous sandstone to completely saturate the sculpted stone rooftops of the great sanctuary of Zion. Rivulets become surface streams that tributary together into what become mighty waterfalls pouring off the edge of cliffs, carrying sand, pebbles, and tree branches into the valley below. The bald pates of Zion's "temples" are streaked red and shiny from washed-out iron. The rusty rocks are furrowed into worry lines, long delicate fingers, peeling alcoves, and dark cavities by rainstorms like this one.

Stunning though the high country is, the heart and soul of Zion National Park is Zion Canyon. The six-mile canyon is a feast for the senses at any time of year, with the park's longest growing season. In April, cottonwoods, oaks, bigtooth maple, velvet ash, and boxelder trees leaf out along the River Walk. Then, in October, long after the high country has drained of color and the last apples been picked from the fruit orchards in Springdale, trees in the canyon are a kaleidoscope of russet, yellow, and gold leaves that dance on autumn winds, fall to the ground in great kickable piles, float in puddles, and stick to hiking boots. In winter, snow dusts the redrocks, freezing the frame on a Currier-and-Ives scene. Ice lingers in side canyons. The appearance of the sun is much appreciated, no longer feared for its summer intensity.

Looking down from on high are enormous cliffs whose Biblical-sounding names evoke the feeling of sanctuary that people have always felt here. The Great White Throne, Court of the Patriarchs, Temple of Sinawava. All are stone masterpieces sculpted from raw rock by the busy little North Fork of the Virgin. The North Fork rises

Checkerboard Mesa and ponderosa pine.
PHOTO© J.C. LEACOCK

Orderville Canyon, a Virgin River tributary, The Narrows.
PHOTO© TOM TILL

on the 10,000-foot-high Markagunt Plateau near Cedar Breaks National Monument and drops a breathtaking 1,300 feet to Zion Canyon through the Zion Narrows—a passageway 2,000-3,000 feet high and barely 35 feet wide.

Water in all its forms shapes the land. It lingers in warm, shallow potholes hollowed out, grain by grain, in sandstone cliffs. It exits as 4,000-year-old springs surrounded by lush riparian vegetation at the base of sandstone cliffs and provides a home for Zion's only endemic animals, the miniscule Zion snail. "When you walk out here," writes naturalist Craig Childs, "you walk the places where water has gone— the canyons, the low places, and the pouroffs. . . . In the desert, water is unedited, perfect."

This unedited desert water attracts a record-breaking 289 bird species, 75 mammal species, 32 reptile and amphibian species, and 800 plant species to Zion—85 percent of all wildlife species found in Utah. In hot, sandy canyon bottoms, desert plants such as pricklypear cactus and sagebrush shelter rabbits and gray foxes. Between elevations of 3,900 feet and 5,500 feet, pygmy forests of piñon and juniper, scrub oak, manzanita, and yucca cling to cliffsides, giving way to stands of ponderosa pine and Gambel oak at around 6,500 feet. At the highest elevations, on the Kolob Plateau, groves of quaking aspen and subalpine fir are the province of mountain lions, condors, and peregrine falcons. On the cool East Rim, Mexican spotted owls and canyon tree frogs live in side canyons between barely petrified Navajo sand dune formations, tessellated by crossbedding and groundwater dripping down through cracks.

The role of water in Zion is celebrated at the park's new visitor center, just inside the South Entrance. Heated by its passive solar design and cooled by innovative twin evaporative towers, the rustic log-and-stone building echoes earlier "parkitecture," blending seamlessly into the Watchman and other cliffs behind it. Outdoor exhibits tell the story of Zion and help visitors with trip planning. Native plant landscaping is irrigated by one of many ditches built by the Civilian Conservation Corps in the 1930s. This channel and others in the park echo the check dams and simple irrigation devices of prehistoric Virgin Anasazi Pueblo builders in Parunuweap Canyon, springs used by later Southern Paiutes to grow corn, and the sophisticated dams and ditches built by pioneer Mormon settlers throughout the Virgin River Valley.

Like animals, humans have been drawn to the year-round water at Zion for millennia. Early American settlers such as Isaac Behunin, along with the Rolfe and Heaps families, settled the mouth of Zion Canyon, hoping to farm in its only flat area, an old lakebed dammed by a rockfall. It was Behunin, a Mormon elder with a long memory of religious persecution, who, in 1863, found refuge here and, echoing the words of Isaiah in the Bible, gave the canyon its name: "The Lord shall comfort Zion: he will comfort all her waste places; and he will make her wilderness like Eden, and her desert like the garden of the Lord." Flooding, rockfalls, earthquakes, and lack of sun eventually drove everyone back to towns along the Virgin River Valley, but local residents continued to use the canyon. In 1900, John Winder im-

West Temple and Towers of the Virgin, dawn.

proved Indian trails to the East Rim and helped David Flanigan build an innovative cable to bring timber down from the high country. In 1930, many Springdale men helped construct the 1.1-mile Zion-Mt. Carmel Tunnel linking the canyon with the East Rim.

Old timers with last names of Gifford, Crawford, Hirschi, and Jake remember how it used to be. Those stories are the focus of the new Human History Museum, which opened in the former park visitor center in early 2002. The History Museum is the first stop on the Zion Shuttle, a propane-powered bus system introduced to serve Zion Canyon and the adjoining town of Springdale in May 2000.

The shuttles have transformed the experience of visiting Zion Canyon. What one notices first is that natural quiet has been returned to the canyon. Instead of engine noise, exhaust fumes, and argumentative voices, there are the happy sounds of playful human beings, the gargling sound of the river, the rush of wind in trees, the *skree* of a red-tailed hawk, the birdlike squeal of a ground squirrel, glimpses of wild turkeys and mule deer roadside.

With no traffic, one can simply walk through the canyon on the paved road and pick up a shuttle at any point. Suddenly, hiking the Emerald Pools, Angels Landing, Echo Canyon, and other canyon trails seems easy and fun. On a summer visit in 2001, I stood in the middle of an empty road at 10 a.m. and was filled with such pleasure, I laughed out loud. The mission of the National Park Service is to both protect the scenery and make it accessible to all of us. In the 21st century, Zion National Park leads the way in doing exactly that.

Great White Throne, Zion Canyon, late afternoon.

◉SIZE: 229 square miles.
◉FOUNDED: Set aside as Mukuntuweap National Monument in 1909. Renamed Zion National Monument in 1918. Upgraded to Zion National Park in 1919. **◉LOCATION:** From west, take Interstate 15 north to Utah 9 turnoff, then continue to park's South Entrance. From east, take US 89 to Mount Carmel Junction. Continue west on Utah 9 to park's East Entrance. **◉ELEVATIONS:** 4,000 feet to 9,000 feet. **◉HIGHLIGHTS:** The Temple of Sinawava, Court of the Patriarchs, Angels Landing, Emerald Pools, Weeping Rock, Riverside Walk, West Temple, the Watchman, Kolob Arch, and Checkerboard Mesa. **◉SEEING THE PARK:** 6-mile Zion Canyon is open to hiking and mountain biking year round; vehicles are now restricted (see Special Considerations below). Other scenic drives include 10-mile Zion-Mt. Carmel Highway to Checkerboard Mesa via the historic 1.1-mile Zion-Mt. Carmel Tunnel (vehicle size restrictions apply); Kolob Terrace Road to Lava Point (closed by snow in winter); 5-mile Kolob Canyons Road from Interstate 15 to the Finger Canyons of the Kolob. Day hikes include the 2-mile paved Riverside Walk (easy), 8-mile Observation Point Trail (strenuous), 2-mile Hidden Canyon Trail (moderate), 5-mile Angels Landing Trail (strenuous), and 2-mile Emerald Pools Trail (moderate) in Zion Canyon; the 2-mile paved Parus Trail along the East Fork of the Virgin (easy); 6-mile Wildcat Canyon Trail (moderate to strenuous) from Kolob Terrace Road; and the 7-mile Kolob Arch Trail (strenuous) from Kolob Canyons Road. **◉VISITOR CENTER:** Zion Canyon Visitor Center at the South Entrance is open 8 a.m. to 5 p.m. year-round, and has park information, outdoor exhibits, publications, backcountry trip planning and permits, seasonal registration for Zion Lodge, parking, main shuttle hub. Smaller Kolob Canyons Visitor Center is open 8 a.m. to 5 p.m. daily year-round (until 7 p.m. in summer) and is accessed from Interstate 15 via Exit 40. **◉VISITOR SERVICES:** Zion Lodge in Zion Canyon has motel-style rooms and historic log cabins; restaurant and snack bar. Springdale, adjoining the park at the South Entrance, has numerous hotels, restaurants, stores. For more information, contact Zion Canyon Chamber of Commerce at 1-888-518-7070 or www.zionpark.com. **◉CAMPGROUNDS:** Watchman Campground has 160 sites; nearby South Campground has 128 sites. Only the Watchman Campground takes reservations; call 1-800-365-2267 or log on to www.reservations.nps.gov on the Internet. Lava Point Primitive Campground has 6 free sites, open May to October; no water. **◉SPECIAL CONSIDERATIONS:** From Easter to Halloween, free shuttles take visitors through Zion Canyon, stopping at 8 scenic points along the way. A second shuttle connects with the park from points throughout Springdale. Buses run from 6 a.m. to 11 p.m.; every 6-10 minutes during peak periods. **◉PARK CONTACT INFORMATION:** Superintendent, Zion National Park, Springdale, UT 84767; 435-772-3256; www.nps.gov/zion.

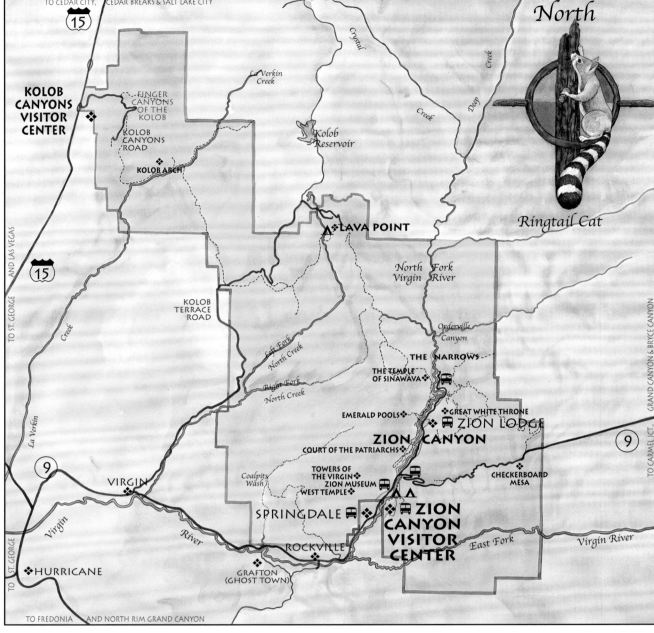

ILLUSTRATION BY DARLECE CLEVELAND

OPPOSITE: *Datura (moonflower) in the Court of the Patriarchs, Zion Canyon.* PHOTO© TOM TILL

The Colorado River at Granite Rapids, Grand Canyon National Park. PHOTO© JEFF D. NICHOLAS

Erosion by the Colorado River is the dominant force in shaping and removing the sedimentary rocks of the Colorado Plateau. Nowhere is this power more evident than in Arizona's million-acre Grand Canyon National Park. Here, within the last 10 million years, like a genie performing an "Open, Sesame!" on Mother Earth, the Colorado River has already spirited away rocks found farther north in Utah's Grand Staircase, then chopped a mile-deep canyon into 12 older rock formations. Fossilized limestones, red sandstones, dark lava rocks, and ancient metamorphic schists are exposed in canyon walls, a geological record dating back 1.8 billion years, the dawn of life on Earth.

Like Canyonlands, the Grand Canyon is a canyon system. The 1,440-mile-long Colorado River, dropping 2,000 feet between Lees Ferry and the Grand Wash Cliffs through a series of whitewater rapids, has carved a 277-mile-long canyon that averages 300 feet wide and 40 feet deep. Tributary streams, rain, ice, wind, and gravity continue to widen the canyon—it is now an amazing 18 miles wide. These secondary erosional forces are responsible for the stunningly beautiful labyrinth of buttes, temples, and sheer cliffs once described by British writer J.B. Priestley as "Beethoven's Ninth Symphony in stone and light."

Grand Canyon's 5 million annual international visitors concentrate at the 7,000-foot South Rim, which has all-weather roads, visitor services, and easy access from nearby Tusayan, Flagstaff, and Williams. Williams also offers daily rides on historic Grand Canyon Railroad steam trains. In the early 1900s, Santa Fe Railroad partnered with concessionaire Fred Harvey to build hotels, restaurants, stores, and galleries still operating today. Between 1904 and 1935, Mary Elizabeth Jane Colter designed Bright Angel Lodge, Hopi House, Lookout Studio, and the Desert Watch Tower, inspired by the Southwest's indigenous materials and cultures.

To really understand the canyon, you'll need to get below the rim. Bright Angel Trail and South Kaibab Trail, blazed by early miners, are the only maintained park trails into the canyon and both require good physical condition and preparation. Mule rides down Bright Angel Trail to Phantom Ranch are popular, but must be booked months ahead. There are many fine overlooks along the East Rim and West Rim Trails and Drives. For those coming from Kanab, Utah, on Highway 89A, the 8,000-foot North Rim is accessible via a 44-mile scenic highway from Jacob Lake (closed by snow between November and May). The historic Grand Canyon Lodge and cabins and campground overlook Bright Angel Canyon; the main canyon can be viewed by taking 23-mile scenic Cape Royal Road.

OPPOSITE: Sunset from South Rim, Grand Canyon National Park. PHOTO© JEFF D. NICHOLAS

CEDAR BREAKS NATIONAL MONUMENT   PHOTO© JEFF D. NICHOLAS

CORAL PINK SAND DUNES STATE PARK   PHOTO© JEFF D. NICHOLAS

DEAD HORSE POINT STATE PARK   PHOTO© JEFF D. NICHOLAS

GOBLIN VALLEY STATE PARK   PHOTO© JEFF D. NICHOLAS

ANASAZI INDIAN STATE PARK

PO Box 1429, Boulder, UT 84716, (435) 355-7308

This Virgin Anasazi pueblo, known as the Coombs site, is in Boulder on Utah 12, adjoining Grand Staircase–Escalante National Monument. Occupied from A.D. 1050 to 1215, it was one of the largest prehistoric Indian communities west of the Colorado River until it burned. The village is largely unexcavated, but many artifacts have been uncovered and are on display in the newly remodeled museum. A self-guided trail and a life-sized six-room replica of an ancient dwelling provide visitors with insight into Ancestral Puebloan lifeways. Picnic sites. No camping.

CEDAR BREAKS NATIONAL MONUMENT

2390 West Highway 56, Suite 11, Cedar City, UT 84720 (435) 586-9451 or www.nps.gov/cebr

This highly eroded amphitheater of orange Claron Formation, on the western edge of the 10,000-foot Markagunt Plateau, was called the Circle of Painted Cliffs by the Southern Paiute. It was renamed by Mormon pioneer ranchers, who noted the lack of "cedar," or juniper, trees in the amphitheater. Steeper, more colorful, and less visited than Bryce Canyon, Cedar Breaks remains pure wilderness. The scenic drive offers photogenic viewpoints. Rim trails lead to 4,000-year-old bristlecones, alpine ponds, and meadows exploding with sunflowers, bluebells, and other high-country bloomers from June to September. Head here for a picnic or campout to escape summer heat in the desert.

CORAL PINK SAND DUNES STATE PARK

PO Box 95, Kanab, UT 84741, (435) 648-2800

Located south of Zion National Park, near Kanab, this 3,700-acre state park preserves pink sand dunes several hundred feet high that eroded from nearby sandstone cliffs and blew into a gap in the Vermilion Cliffs. The dunes have unique plant and animals adapted to the deep sandy environment, which may be viewed from trails crossing the dunes. There is a popular 22-site campground, a resident ranger, and separate areas for hiking and off-road vehicles. Photographers won't want to miss sunset here.

DEAD HORSE POINT STATE PARK

PO Box 609, Moab, UT 84532-0609

(435) 259-2614 or (800) 322-3770 (camping res.)

Located next to the Island in the Sky District of Canyonlands, this 5,250-acre state park has breathtaking eastern views of the La Sal Mountains, eroded cliffs, mesas, buttes, and river canyons. At the base of the 2,000-foot mesa is an enormous horseshoe bend, or entrenched meander, in the Colorado River. Dead Horse Point itself is a sandstone peninsula separated by a 30-yard-wide "neck." According to legend, it was used as a corral by turn-of-the-century ranchers. On one occasion, for some forgotten reason, horses were left corralled here without water and died of thirst, hence the name. The park has 10 miles of rim trails and a 21-site campground with developed facilities.

EDGE OF THE CEDARS STATE PARK MUSEUM

660 West 400 North, Blanding, UT 84511-4000

(435) 678-2238

This not-to-be-missed cultural park preserves the remains of a major Ancestral Puebloan village and great kiva dating from A.D. 825 to 1220. The museum serves as the archaeological repository for southeastern Utah and has modern research and artifact processing areas. A large quantity of prehistoric pottery uncovered in the area is housed here, with a number of pieces on display. State-of-the-art, multimedia exhibits interpret the prehistoric Ancestral Puebloan and modern Ute and Navajo cultures. There are native plant and sculpture gardens, picnic areas, but no camping.

GLEN CANYON NATIONAL RECREATION AREA

PO Box 1507, Page, AZ 86040

(520) 608-6404 or www.nps.gov/glca

The completion of Glen Canyon Dam on the Colorado River in 1963 created 1,961-square-mile Lake Powell, flooding most of Glen Canyon itself. The soaring cliffs surrounding the lake are beautifully eroded Navajo Sandstone, but many more intricate geological features now lie beneath the lake, along with thousands of Ancestral Pueblo sites. Explore the dam at Page, Arizona; rent a houseboat; or take a boat trip and visit the mid-lake region at Bullfrog and Halls Crossing. Many of the lake's 96 side canyons are only accessible by boat and provide unique hiking opportunities.

GOBLIN VALLEY STATE PARK

PO Box 637, Green River, UT 84525-0637

(435) 564-3633

Located between Hanksville and Green River, Goblin Valley State Park preserves thousands of bizarre

"goblins," spires, and balanced rocks, or hoodoos, which erosion has sculpted from soft Entrada Sandstone. Trails lead to hoodoos, old mines, and views of the Henry Mountains, the Maze, and the San Rafael Swell, a dramatic monocline that runs behind the park. The 21-unit, developed campground is popular with park travelers.

GRAND STAIRCASE–ESCALANTE NATIONAL MONUMENT

PO Box 246, Escalante, UT 84726

(435) 826-5499 or www.ut.blm.gov/monument

Set aside in 1996, this 1.9-million-acre national monument was the first to be administered by the Bureau of Land Management. It is an undeveloped landscape monument, emphasizing scientific research over visitation. There are three separate units. The Grand Staircase, east of Kanab, preserves and interprets the geological feature of the same name as well as local Mormon culture. The rugged Kaiparowits Plateau—Zane Grey's fictitious Wild Horse Mesa—is remote and rarely visited, a place where scientists are uncovering unique Mesozoic-era fossils and American Indian artifacts in an area once slated for coal mining. Most visitors head for the Escalante Canyons, where backpackers can wander for days through the glorious tangle of sandstone slot canyons carved by the lushly vegetated Escalante River. Paved scenic roads include U.S. Highways 12 and 89, Johnson Canyon, and the Burr Trail. The monument backcountry is also accessed by dirt roads to Cottonwood Canyon and Hole in the Rock. Visitor centers in the outlying communities of Kanab, Escalante, Big Water, and Boulder have information on trip planning, overnight backcountry permits, interpretive exhibits, and publications. Two primitive campgrounds are located at Calf and Deer Creeks.

HOVENWEEP NATIONAL MONUMENT

McElmo Route, Cortez, CO 81321

(970) 562-4282 or www.nps.gov/hove

Six 12th- and 13th-century Mesa Verde-style Ancestral Pueblo buildings, built in unusual round, square, and D-shaped towers, line the rim of Little Ruin Canyon at this 1.2-square-mile national monument on Cajon Mesa, between Blanding, Utah, and Cortez, Colorado. Two short rim trails lead from the new visitor center and campground to Square Tower Group, Hovenweep Castle, and other structures used by prehistoric farmers.

MONUMENT VALLEY NAVAJO TRIBAL PARK

PO Box 360289, Monument Valley, UT 84536

(435) 727-3353 or 727-3287

Monument Valley isn't a valley at all but the Monument Upwarp, a geological uplift of strangely eroded de Chelly Sandstone and crumbly Organ Rock Shale stretching from Comb Ridge and the San Juan River in the north to Monument Valley and Black Mesa in the south. From the visitor center, a 17-mile dirt road leads to 11 spectacular vistas of the Mittens, Totem Pole, Full Moon Arch, and other formations made famous in John Ford Westerns like *Stagecoach*. Horseback, Jeep, and van tours emphasize prehistoric Pueblo culture and the contemporary traditional way of life of Navajo residents. They can be arranged at the visitor center or Goulding's Lodge, the inn started by trader Harry Goulding and his wife "Mike" in the 1930s.

NATURAL BRIDGES NATIONAL MONUMENT

PO Box 1, Lake Powell, UT 84533

(435) 692-1234 or www.nps.gov/nabr

This 11.9-square-mile national monument, south of Canyonlands, was the first to be set aside in Utah in 1906. It preserves three dramatic Cedar Mesa Sandstone natural bridges carved by tributaries of the Colorado River. At 220 feet, Sipapu Bridge is second only in size to nearby Rainbow Bridge. Visitors may hike canyon bottoms to view Sipapu, Kachina, and Owachomo Bridges, or view them from above on nine-mile Bridge View Drive, along with Horsecollar Ruin, a small 12th-century Ancestral Pueblo ruin that shows both Kayenta and Mesa Verde influences. The 13-site campground is a hidden gem. The visitor center is housed in one of the first solar-powered buildings in the National Park System.

RAINBOW BRIDGE NATIONAL MONUMENT

PO Box 1507, Page, AZ 86040

(520) 608-6200 or www.nps.gov/rabr

At a height of 309 feet, Rainbow Bridge is the largest known natural bridge in the world. Carved by Bridge Creek, a tributary of the Colorado River, the span is composed of 200-million-year-old Navajo Sandstone underlaid by slightly older Kayenta Formation. Travelers can reach the site by boat from marinas at Dangling Rope, Wahweap, Bullfrog, or Halls Crossing on Lake Powell, or on foot or horseback (permit required) over Navajo tribal land. The bridge is sacred to the Navajo.

DUNES AT MONUMENT VALLEY NAVAJO TRIBAL PARK   PHOTO© TOM TILL

HOVENWEEP NATIONAL MONUMENT   PHOTO© JEFF D. NICHOLAS

NATURAL BRIDGES NATIONAL MONUMENT   PHOTO© TOM TILL

RAINBOW BRIDGE NATIONAL MONUMENT   PHOTO© TOM TILL

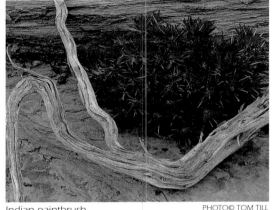

Indian paintbrush　　PHOTO© TOM TILL

Claret cup cactus　　PHOTO© STEVE MULLIGAN

Prince's plume　　PHOTO© BRUCE JACKSON/Gnass Photo Images

All of North America's life zones are found in Canyon Country, a result of its 4,000- to 12,000-foot span in elevation, along with differing temperatures, rocks, soils, slope angles, exposures, and availability of water. The canyon-and-mesa topography of the Colorado Plateau encourages diversity. More than 80 percent of all plants in Utah are found in Zion National Park, for example, and 340 plant species live nowhere else, with 80 endemic species listed or recommended for federal listing as threatened and endangered.

Plants must somehow find water, stop it from escaping, and attract pollinators to ensure reproduction. Many have bright blooms and heavy pollen centers to lure moths, butterflies, bees, beetles, bats, and birds. Desert plants often grow long roots to tap underground water sources or, like cacti, use a large, shallow root network to suck up rainfall when it arrives. Broad leaves are a liability in a desert. Plants

either reduce the size and number; shed them during the hottest times of year, like brittlebrush; develop curly, hairy, or waxy leaves (buffaloberry has silvery-gray hairs on the underside of thick leaves to keep cool); turn the leaves toward or away from the sun throughout the day, as does red-barked manzanita, a high-country shrub; or, like pricklypear, a cactus common throughout the plateau due to its ability to withstand hard freezes, convert leaves to spines, photosynthesize food through exposed pads, and use its spines as protection.

Evergreens provide a soothing green counterpoint to bare sandstone and hardened lava. Instead of leaves, conifers have waxy needles, a useful way of minimizing water loss, protecting the tree from temperature fluctuations (100 degrees in summer to single digits in winter), and shrugging off snow. Drought makes for shorter, thinner trees, and many have special adaptations. Gnarled bristlecones live up to 4,000 years by allowing parts of the tree to die

during extreme drought and by colonizing 9,000-foot canyon rims at Bryce Canyon, a niche trees in the adjoining spruce-fir forest find too hostile. Ponderosa, found in airy stands called "parks" at 6,500 to 8,000 feet, rely on frequent, low-intensity natural fires to open cones and spread seed. The signature conifers are dwarf piñons and junipers, found from 4,000 feet to 6,500 feet. These trees send roots down into joints in sandstone cliffs and are often the only plants able to colonize such steep areas.

Since the late 1800s, junipers (locally called "cedars") have migrated down to mid-elevation grasslands once belly-high to a horse with sideoats grama, needle-and-thread, and other native grasses. Overgrazing, erosion, the invasion of junipers as well as such shrubs as rabbitbrush, snakeweed, and greasewood, along with the arrival of a ruthless competitor, the exotic annual cheatgrass, have sounded the death knell for Colorado Plateau grasslands, probably forever. Abundant native grasses are

Giant helleborine　　PHOTO© LARRY ULRICH

Colorado four o'clock　　PHOTO© JEFF D. NICHOLAS

Spiderwort　　PHOTO© JEFF D. NICHOLAS

Mule's ears and cryptantha · PHOTO© LARRY ULRICH

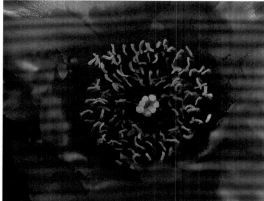

Beavertail cactus · PHOTO© JEFF D. NICHOLAS

Rabbitbrush · PHOTO© JEFF D. NICHOLAS

now only found in places like the Needles District of the Canyonlands and ungrazed areas. The pungent smell of sagebrush after a rain is one of the Southwest's most evocative smells, but wherever plants form a monoculture, biodiversity in an ecosystem once protected by its isolation is lost, affecting humans as well as native wildlife.

The biggest surprise for most visitors to Canyon Country is the sheer numbers of wildflowers, which put on a remarkable display in the years following good winter rains. Flowers are found at every elevation and survive by employing varied strategies. Woody and hairy stems keep water in and help flowers survive temperature extremes. Morning glories, sacred datura, primroses, and flax open at night or in early morning so that they can be pollinated by moths or bats, but close in the heat of the day. Paintbox red Indian paintbrush, a semi-parasitic plant whose red flowers are really sepals hiding the knife-shaped green flower in-

side, blooms throughout Canyon Country. At low elevations, it pops out of cracks in the desert sandstone. When the snow melts in the high country, it can be found in alpine meadows alongside carpets of bluebells, purple lupines, sunflowers, purple asters, penstemon, scarlet gilia, and other flowers that must bloom, pollinate, and reproduce before fall snows arrive. Some flowers prefer soils with particular minerals. Yellow-wanded prince's plume, a mustard, likes the Chinle Formation, which has abundant selenium, a substitute for nitrogen. When miners saw prince's plume growing, they knew that uranium was nearby. Spring-blooming milkvetch, a legume, is another selenium-lover. Endemic milkvetches are found in Zion and Capitol Reef National Parks.

Rivers, waterfalls, and seeps attract plants that need to get their feet wet. The most magical places are hanging gardens of columbine, shooting star, fern, and other plants hidden at the bottoms of Navajo Sandstone canyons.

Netleaf hackberry, velvet ash, boxelder, and coyote willow throng riverways, alongside a poplar, the Fremont cottonwood. Large cottonwoods provide important nesting habitat for birds, bats, and other animals. They grow fast and die after a century or so, and, like willows, require a broad floodplain to germinate new seedlings. This creates problems where rivers have been rechanneled to prevent flooding, such as in Zion Canyon. In that park, a new program is working to find ways to balance flood control with important cottonwood regeneration. Land managers are also looking for ways to eradicate another exotic plant choking waterways: tamarisk, or saltcedar. An Asian ornamental tree, tamarisk was introduced in the late 1800s to stabilize eroded riverbanks; however, it outcompetes native willows and cottonwoods by producing more seeds, germinating faster, excreting salts that kill grasses and seedlings, and sucking up and transpiring 300 to 400 gallons of water a day per tree.

Aspen trunks · PHOTO© JEFF D. NICHOLAS

Vine-leaf maple · PHOTO© JEFF D. NICHOLAS

Fremont cottonwood · PHOTO© JEFF D. NICHOLAS

Coyote   PHOTO© FRED HIRSCHMANN

Mountain lion   PHOTO© TOM & PAT LEESON

Gray fox   PHOTO© TOM & PAT LEESON

Desert country seems quiet during the day because many animals are nocturnal, sensibly keeping cool underground in the day, then emerging at night to hunt and drink at water holes. The most visible animals are, therefore, birds, which can simply fly away to a better location. The signature bird of the Colorado Plateau is the raven, the largest member of the crow family. Ravens are playful, funny, creative, and intelligent. Working in pairs, they'll steal food from your backpack when you're not looking, scold you in any one of 30 different tones of voice, and put on a remarkable aerial show. Equally vocal are sky-blue Steller's and pinyon jays, which bully smaller seed-eating birds like finches in the piñon-juniper and ponderosa pine forests. The Steller's crest distinguishes it from the piñon jay.

Birds flock to the rivers, where dense foliage provides nesting habitat, protective cover, and easy access to insects and fish. Commonly heard but rarely seen is the canyon wren, a little brown bird with a cocked tail and curved bill. The wren's song—a cascade of descending notes echoing in sandstone canyons—is one of the most haunting and recognizable in all Canyon Country. White-throated swifts and violet-green swallows make mud homes in cliff alcoves and dart down to the river, hunting for insects. Swifts and swallows are favorite prey for peregrine falcons. Now recovered enough to be removed from listing as a federally endangered species, peregrine falcons nest in high cliffs in Zion and Bryce Canyon and dive at speeds of up to 200 miles per hour.

With their large wingspans, raptors easily fly long distances over rugged country. Red-tailed hawks circle above meadows hoping to snag hare-like jackrabbits as they bolt from bushes. Red-headed turkey vultures search for dead prey, or carrion, like their larger relatives, California condors, an endangered species reintroduced near Grand Canyon National Park's North Rim and now seen frequently in Zion and Bryce Canyon National Parks. Since the Colorado River was dammed, bald eagles have become frequent visitors, fishing for non-native trout now found in the icy waters below the dams. But colder conditions have sounded the death knell for humpback chub, Colorado squawfish, and other native fish, now listed as endangered.

Mule deer browse along roadsides in national parks at dusk, protected from their main predator, mountain lions, by human presence. Secretive mountain lions, or cougars, are found wherever there are elk and deer—they also prey on reintroduced desert bighorn sheep in Zion and Arches National Parks—but their numbers are now much reduced, due to habitat loss and fragmentation as well as overtrapping in the 20th century. Individual cougars travel up to 100 miles nightly. Coyote packs have large hunting circuits, too. These

Mule deer buck   PHOTO© GLENN VAN NIMWEGEN

Mountain bluebird   PHOTO© TOM & PAT LEESON

Badger   PHOTO© TOM & PAT LEESON

Desert bighorns PHOTO© FRANK S. BALTHIS

Ravens PHOTO© RANDI HIRSCHMANN

Immature red-tailed hawk PHOTO© GLENN VAN NIMWEGEN

small members of the dog family eat cotton-tails, jackrabbits, squirrels, and even pets, so keep Fluffie inside at night. They communicate with eerie howls, high-pitched yips, and barks.

At night in the side canyons of Zion and Capitol Reef, you may hear a strange sheeplike bleating. It could be a desert bighorn, but more likely is the odd canyon tree frog, which hangs out on rocks beside pools. Amphibians such as tree frogs, newts, salamanders, red-spotted toads, leopard frogs, and Woodhouse's toads share water-filled pockets in the rocks, known as potholes, with waterstriders, dragonflies, and up to a dozen species of tiny shrimp, snails, and other microfauna, some of which can undergo extreme dessication and still survive. When potholes dry out, toads hop away or, like the spadefoot, cover themselves in protective mucous and dig into the bottom of the pothole to wait for rain.

One desert animal that needs no water at all is Merriam's kangaroo rat. Named for its long hind legs, it recycles all its water from seeds. Rodents are the most plentiful small mammals on the Colorado Plateau. Some live only on isolated buttes in Canyonlands. Others, such as the Abert and Kaibab tassel-eared squirrels, evolved into different species when the Colorado River cut the Grand Canyon through their home. The endangered Utah prairie dog is found only at Bryce Canyon. Most common are cute golden-mantled and antelope ground squirrels and chipmunks. They dine well on acorns, nuts, seeds, cactus, agave, and other native foods, so don't feed them. Human food makes wild animals dependent and willing to risk harm to themselves to obtain it. Rodents also give nasty bites and can carry plague.

Snakes and lizards are commonly found in desert scrub, basking in the sun on rocks early in the morning, keeping cool under brush in the daytime, and hunting in the early evening for rodents, insects, sometimes their own kind. Startled lizards will do pushups in order to appear larger and scare you away. Don't grab them by the tail. It will detach in your hand, allowing the lizard to escape, but leaving it seriously weakened because it lives on the fat in the tail. The tail will grow back eventually, but why subject animals to this harassment? Western whiptail lizards have the longest tails, which they swish back and forth as they run. Plateau lizards range from brown to rose to gray patterns. Most beautiful are collared lizards, which measure 8-12 inches and have a blue-green body and black-and-white collar. Yes, there are snakes, too. Some of the most common are fast-moving whipsnakes, yellow-bellied racers, and Great Basin gopher snakes. Remember: this is their home; you are the visitor. Watch for their presence, keep out of their way, and don't aggravate or try to harm them.

Cactus wren PHOTO© FRANK S. BALTHIS

Collared lizard PHOTO© CAROL POLICH

Bobcat PHOTO© FRANK S. BALTHIS

PAGE 60/61: Archangel Cascades, Right Fork of North Creek, Zion National Park. PHOTO© TOM TILL

RESOURCES AND INFORMATION

EMERGENCY & MEDICAL:
24-HOUR EMERGENCY MEDICAL SERVICE
Dial 911

ROAD CONDITIONS:
ARIZONA	(888) 411-7623
COLORADO	(303) 639-1111
NEVADA	(702) 486-3116
NEW MEXICO	(800) 432-4269
UTAH	(800) 492-2400

MORE INFORMATION:
NATIONAL PARKS ON THE INTERNET:
www.nps.gov

BUREAU OF LAND MANAGEMENT
www.ut.blm.gov/

UTAH STATE PARKS
1636 West North Temple
Salt Lake City, UT 84116
(801) 538-7720
www.parks.state.ut.us/parks/

ARIZONA STRIP INTERPRETIVE ASSOCIATION
345 East Riverside Drive
St. George, UT 84790
(435) 688-3275

BRYCE CANYON NAT'L HIST. ASSOCIATION
PO Box 170002
Bryce Canyon, UT 84717
(435) 834-5322
www.nps.gov/brca

CANYONLANDS NATURAL HISTORY ASSOCIATION
3031 South Highway 191
Moab, UT 84532
(435) 259-6003
www.cnha.org

CAPITOL REEF NATURAL HISTORY ASSOCIATION
HC 70, Box 15
Torrey, UT 84775
(435) 425-3791
www.nps.gov/care/nha

COLORADO NATIONAL MONUMENT ASSOCIATION
Colorado National Monument
Fruita, CO 81521
(970) 858-3617
www.nps.gov/colm

DINOSAUR NATURE ASSOCIATION
1291 East Highway 40, Vernal, UT 84078
(435) 789-8807
www.dinosaurnature.com

DIXIE INTERPRETIVE ASSOCIATION
PO Box 349
Santa Clara, UT 84765
(435) 347-5765

GLEN CANYON NATURAL HISTORY ASSOCIATION
PO Box 1835
Page, AZ 86040
(928) 608-6358
www.glencanyonassociation.org

GRAND CANYON NATIONAL PARK
PO Box 129
Grand Canyon, AZ 86023
(928) 638-7888
www.nps.gov/grca

GRAND CANYON ASSOCIATION
PO Box 399
Grand Canyon, AZ 86023
(928) 638-2481
www.grandcanyon.org

MESA VERDE MUSEUM ASSOCIATION
PO Box 38
Mesa Verde National Park, CO 81330
(970) 529-4445
www.mesaverde.org

PETRIFIED FOREST MUSEUM ASSOCIATION
PO Box 2277
Petrified Forest National Park, AZ 86028
(928) 524-6228
www.cybertrails.com/~pfma

PUBLIC LANDS INTERPRETIVE ASSOCIATION
6501 N. Fourth Street NW
Albuquerque, NM 87107
(505) 345-9498
www.publiclands.org

ZION NATURAL HISTORY ASSOCIATION
Zion National Park, UT 84767
(435) 772-3265
www.zionpark.org

LODGING INSIDE THE PARKS:
ARCHES NATIONAL PARK
No lodging available within the park.

BRYCE CANYON NATIONAL PARK
AMFAC PARKS & RESORTS
14001 E. Iliff, Suite 600
Aurora, CO 80014
(303) 29 -PARKS
www.amfac.com

CANYONLANDS NATIONAL PARK
No lodging available within the park.

CAPITOL REEF NATIONAL PARK
No lodging available within the park.

ZION NATIONAL PARK
AMFAC PARKS & RESORTS
14001 E. Iliff, Suite 600
Aurora, CO 80014
(303) 29 -PARKS
www.amfac.com

CAMPING INSIDE THE PARKS:
Phone: (800) 365-CAMP (2267),
On the Internet: www.reservations.nps.gov

UTAH STATE PARK CAMPING
(800) 322-3770

LODGING OUTSIDE THE PARKS:
UTAH TRAVEL COUNCIL
Council Hall
Salt Lake City, UT 84114
(801) 538-1030
www.utah.com

CANYONLANDS TRAVEL REGION
40 N. 100 East/PO Box 550
Moab, UT 84532
(800) 635-6622
and
117 S. Main
Monticello, UT 84535
(800) 574-4386

CASTLE COUNTRY TRAVEL REGION
906 N. 1400 West/PO Box 1550
St. George, UT 84771
(800) 233-8824

COLOR COUNTRY TRAVEL REGION
PO Box 1550
St. George, UT 84771
(800) 233-8824
www.utahscolorcountry.org

DINOSAURLAND TRAVEL REGION
25 E. Main
Vernal, UT 84078
(800) 477-5558

PANORAMALAND TRAVEL REGION
4 S. Main/PO Box 71
Nephi, UT 84648
(800) 748-4361

OTHER REGIONAL SITES:
CANYON de CHELLY NATIONAL MONUMENT
PO Box 588
Chinle, AZ 86503
www.nps.gov/cach

COLORADO NATIONAL MONUMENT
Fruita, CA 81521
(970) 858-3617
www.nps.gov/colm

DINOSAUR NATIONAL MONUMENT
4545 E. Highway 40
Dinosaur, CO 81610
(435) 789-2115
www.nps.gov/dino

ESCALANTE STATE PARK
710 North Reservoir Road
Escalante, UT 84726
(435) 826-4466

FREMONT INDIAN STATE PARK
11550 West Clear Creek Canyon Rd.
Sevier, UT 84766
(435) 527-4631

GOOSENECKS STATE PARK
PO Box 788
Blanding, UT 84511
(435) 678-2238

HUBBELL TRADING POST NATIONAL HISTORIC SITE
PO Box 150
Ganado, AZ 86505
(928) 755-3405
www.nps.gov/hutr

KODACHROME BASIN STATE PARK
PO Box 238
Cannonville, UT 84718
(435) 678562

LAKE MEAD NATIONAL RECREATION AREA
601 Nevada Highway
Boulder City, NV 89005-2426
(702) 293-8907
www.nps.gov/lame

MESA VERDE NATIONAL PARK
PO Box 8
Mesa Verde National Park, CO 81330
(970) 529-4465, 529-4633 (TDD)
www.nps.gov/meve

NAVAJO NATIONAL MONUMENT
HC-71, Box 3
Tonalea, AZ 86044
(928) 672-2700
www.nps.gov/nava

PETRIFIED FOREST NATIONAL PARK
PO Box 2217
Petrified Forest National Park, AZ 86028
(928) 524-6228
www.nps.gov/pefo

PIPE SPRING NATIONAL MONUMENT
HC 65, Box 5
Fredonia, AZ 86022
(928) 643-7105
www.nps.gov/pisp

SNOW CANYON STATE PARK
PO Box 140
Santa Clara, UT 84765
(435) 628-2255

TIMPANOGOS CAVE NAT'L MONUMENT
RR 3, Box 200
American Fork, UT 84003
(801) 756-5238
www.nps.gov/tica

WUPATKI NATIONAL MONUMENT
HC 33, Box 444A, #14
Flagstaff, AZ 86004
(928) 679-2365
www.nps.gov/wupa

SUGGESTED READING:

Abbey, Edward. *Desert Solitaire*. (1968). Reprint. New York, NY: Ballantine Books. 1971.

Aitchison, Stewart. *Grand Canyon National Park*. Mariposa, CA: Sierra Press. 1999.

Anasazi Architecture and American Design. Edited by Baker H. Morrow and V.B. Price. Albuquerque, NM: University of New Mexico Press. 1997.

Baars, Donald L. *The Colorado Plateau: A Geologic History. Revised Edition*. Albuquerque, NM: University of New Mexico Press. 2000.

Brady, Irene. *The Redrock Canyon Explorer: A Virtual Visit to an Imaginary Canyon*. Talent, OR: Nature Works Explorer Library Series. 2000.

Buchanan, Hayle. *Wildflowers of Southwestern Utah: A Field Guide to Bryce Canyon, Cedar Breaks, and Surrounding Plant Communities*. Bryce Canyon, UT: Bryce Canyon Natural History Association. 1992.

Chesher, Greer. *Bryce Canyon: The Desert's Hoodoo Heart*. Mariposa, CA: Sierra Press. 2000.

Chesher, Greer K. *Grand Staircase–Escalante National Monument: Heart of the Desert Wild*. Bryce Canyon, UT: Bryce Canyon Natural History Association. 2000.

Childs, Craig. *The Secret Knowledge of Water: Discovering the Essence of the American Desert*. Seattle, WA: Sasquatch Books. 2000.

DeBuys, William. *Seeing Things Whole: The Essential John Wesley Powell*. San Francisco, CA: Island Press. 2001.

Fontana, Bernard. *A Guide to Contemporary Southwest Indians*. Tucson, AZ: Southwest Parks and Monuments Association.1999

Frost, Kent, with Rosalie Goldman. *My Canyonlands*. Monticello, UT: Canyon country Publications. 1997.

Hafen, Lyman. *Mukuntuweap: Landscape and Story in Zion Canyon*. St. George, UT: Tonaquint Press. 1996.

Hamilton, Wayne. *The Sculpturing of Zion*. Revised edition. Springdale, UT: Zion Natural History Association.1992.

Hinchman, Sandra. *Hiking the Southwest's Canyon Country*. Seattle, WA: The Mountaineers Books. 1997.

Leach, Nicky. *Arches and Canyonlands National Parks*. Mariposa, CA: Sierra Press. 1997.

Leach, Nicky. *Cedar Breaks National Monument*. Springdale, UT: Zion Natural History Association. 1994.

Leach, Nicky. *The Guide to National Parks of the Southwest*. Tucson, AZ: Southwest Parks and Monuments Association. 1982.

Leach, Nicky. *Next to the Throne of God: Kolob Canyons, Zion National Park*. Springdale, UT: Zion Natural History Association. 1994

Leach, Nicky. *Zion National Park: Sanctuary In The Desert*. Mariposa, CA: Sierra Press. 1999.

Lister, Robert and Florence. *Those Who Came Before: Southwest Archaeology in the National Park System*. Tucson, AZ: Southwest Parks and Monuments Association. 1989.

Lopez, Barry Holstun. *Desert Notes: Reflections in the Eye of a Raven*. New York, NY: Avon Books. 1976.

Melloy, Ellen. *Raven's Exile: A Season on the Green River*. New York, NY: Henry Holt. 1994.

Nabhan, Gary Paul and Stephen Trimble. *The Geography of Childhood: Why Children Need Wild Places*. Boston, MA: Beacon Press. 1994.

Roberts, David. *In Search of the Old Ones: Exploring the Anasazi World of the Southwest*. New York, NY: Touchstone Books. 1997.

Roylance, Ward A. *The Enchanted Wilderness: A Redrock Odyssey*. Torrey, UT: Four Corners West Publishing. 1986.

Rusho, W.L. *Everett Reuss: A Vagabond for Beauty*. Salt Lake City, UT: Gibbs Smith Publishers. 1983.

Russell, Sharman Apt. *Anatomy of a Rose: Exploring the Secret Life of Flowers*. Cambridge, MA: Perseus Publishing. 2001.

Stegner, Wallace. *Mormon Country*. Lincoln, NE: University of Nebraska Press. 1970.

Tales of Canyonlands Cowboys. Edited by Richard F. Negri. Logan, UT: Utah State University Press. 1997.

Welsh, Stanley. *Wildflowers of Zion National Park*. Springdale, UT: Zion Natural History Association. 1990.

Williams, David. *A Naturalist's Guide to Canyon Country*. Helena, MT: Falcon Press in cooperation with Canyonlands Natural History Association. 2000.

Williams, Terry Tempest. *An Unspoken Hunger: Stories From the Field*. New York, NY: Vintage Books. 1994.

Wilkinson, Charles. *Fire on the Plateau: Conflict and Endurance in the American Southwest*. San Francisco, CA: Island Press. 1999.

Woodbury, Angus. *A History of Southern Utah and its National Parks*. Springdale, UT: Zion Natural History Association. 1997.

ACKNOWLEDGMENTS

Special thanks to Gayle Pollock at Bryce Canyon Natural History Association, Brad Wallis at Canyonlands NHA, Shirley Torgerson at Capitol Reef NHA, Lyman Hafen at Zion NHA, and Pam Frazier at Grand Canyon Association, and their staffs for their support, encouragement, and assistance and all the talented photographers who made their imagery available for use in this book.

—JDN

PRODUCTION CREDITS

Publisher: Jeff D. Nicholas
Author: Nicky Leach
Editor: Richard Mahler
Production Assistant: Marcia Huskey
Illustrations: Darlece Cleveland
Printing Coordination: Sung In Printing America

ISBN 10: 1-58071-046-8
ISBN 13: 978-1-58071-046-6
©2002 Panorama International Productions, Inc.

SIERRA PRESS
4988 Gold Leaf Drive, Mariposa, CA 95338
Visit our Website:
WWW.NationalParksUSA.com

OPPOSITE
The Fiery Furnace and La Sal Mountains, Arches National Park. PHOTO© TOM TILL
BELOW
Hoodoo in Goblin Valley State Park.
PHOTO© JEFF D. NICHOLAS